Get Messy
Art

Get Messy Art

The No-Rules, No-Judgment, No-Pressure Approach to Making Art

CAYLEE GREY

QUARRY

Inspiring | Educating | Creating | Entertaining

Brimming with creative inspiration, how-to projects, and useful information to enrich your everyday life, quarto.com is a favorite destination for those pursuing their interests and passions.

First Published in 2022 by Quarry Books, an imprint of The Quarto Group, 100 Cummings Center, Suite 265-D, Beverly, MA 01915, USA. T (978) 282-9590 F (978) 283-2742 Quarto.com

Quarry Books titles are also available at discount for retail, wholesale, promotional, and bulk purchase. For details, contact the Special Sales Manager by email at specialsales@quarto.com or by mail at The Quarto Group, Attn: Special Sales Manager, 100 Cummings Center, Suite 265-D, Beverly, MA 01915, USA.

ISBN: 978-0-7603-7116-9

Digital edition published in 2022
eISBN: 978-0-7603-7117-6

Library of Congress Cataloging-in-Publication Data

Names: Grey, Caylee, author.
Title: Get messy art : the no-rules, no-judgment, and no-pressure approach to making art / Caylee Grey.
Description: [Beverly] : Quarry, [2021] | Includes index. | Summary:
   "Forget perfection-grab your supplies and get messy with the easy
   techniques and projects for creating with watercolor, acrylic, markers,
   inks, and more in Get Messy Art. Play, experiment, and explore with zero
   judgment, zero pressure, and all the fun"-- Provided by publisher.
Identifiers: LCCN 2021033384 (print) | LCCN 2021033385 (ebook) | ISBN xxxxxxxxxxxxx (trade paperback) | ISBN 9780760371176 (ebook)
Subjects: LCSH: Handicraft. | Scrapbook journaling. | Mixed media (Art)--Technique.
Classification: LCC TT857 .G74 2021 (print) | LCC TT857 (ebook) | DDC 745.5--dc23
LC record available at https://lccn.loc.gov/2021033384
LC ebook record available at https://lccn.loc.gov/2021033385

Design: Allison Meierding
Photography: Natalie Roessler

To the perfectionist who chooses mess instead.

Contents

Introduction

Welcome to this book. You're going to love it.

But—I'll tell you this up front—you need to do the work.

Reading these words might make you feel all warm and fuzzy inside, but once you turn them into action, they will light a fire inside you.

This book is the catalyst, but it's up to you to turn that spark into a blazing flame.

I, along with the incredible artists in this book, have done a massive chunk of the work. Almost all of it. We've learned the lessons, we've put in the time, we've articulated it all. There's just a tiny bit of work left to do, and it is yours. It may feel big and insurmountable, but you can do big things.

I'd like to introduce myself. I'm Caylee Grey, and I hope you put on a thick South African accent as you read this. My favorite title ever given to me is Fairy Artmother. Other favorites include wife and mama. I facilitate the online Get Messy art journaling community. For the past seven years, I've been happily swishing and flicking my artsy wand as I help fellow creative humans just like you embrace the mess and magic of a fulfilling, creative life.

I'm a South African living out my dream on the edge of a forest in Germany. I have horrible taste in music but spectacular taste in humans, which is why I'm so happy you're reading this. You're clearly great.

My art journaling adventure began as a way for me to get messy, ditch perfectionism, stay accountable, and consistently create art. But, magically, it transformed into something so much more than that.

Years ago, a friend and I committed to making art journaling a habit—even though we had yet to create a page. And for some reason it worked. Others joined us, and the momentum built. This turned into Get Messy, the most amazing community with more than three thousand members making things every day.

The best part is that I'm not finished. Doing things makes me want to do more.

I'm overenthusiastic by nature, so I'm incredibly excited to hand this over to you. I'm keen to see you take the lessons and projects in this book and turn them into art. Your creative journey tickles me pink—both the beautiful parts and the messy bits. Especially the messy bits. Please share your projects on Instagram so I can see them, and so others reading this book can be inspired by you. Just use the hashtag #getmessybook to join in.

That's your first action step. Throughout this book, you'll see that I quite like action steps. I'm fond of practical, tangible things. I'm also fond of sharing. I'd love for you to do both at each step.

Now, let's get messy!

The Messy Movement

Before we get started on what a Messy Artist is, I'd like to touch on just being an artist. *My* definition of an artist is someone who makes art.

You do not have to be good or prolific. You do not have to share or sell your work. Your art does not need to look like the stuff hanging in museums. Good or bad art, newly creating or fifty years into your creative journey, you're an artist. If you make art, you're an artist.

Do not dare doubt yourself—unless you're not making art, in which case, make some art and call yourself an artist.

The Messy Artist goes a step deeper, looking inside and questioning everything they've been taught in exchange for freedom.

That might sound dramatic, but being a Messy Artist is not just something you do when you schedule your creative time. Being a Messy Artist is all-encompassing; being a Messy Artist is disagreeing with the world's take on perfection.

Encouraging others to be messy is my life's work.

THE MESSY MANIFESTO

At Get Messy, we have a manifesto made up of six pillars on which we build our creative lives. This manifesto is your official invitation to live as a Messy Artist.

As a community, we believe in:

- **THE MESS:** We believe that we grow through play, learn through practice, and that creation comes from embracing the beauty of the *messy middle*. The only thing not invited to this party? Perfectionism. Leave that guy at the gate.

- **THE HABIT:** We believe that the starving artist myth needs to die (kindly but quickly), and that quality comes through quantity. To do our best, we need to be willing to do the work, hustle, and turn dreams into habits that we engage in every single day.

- **CONNECTION THROUGH COMMUNITY:** We believe that being a creative soul can be lonely, which is why we believe in support, and in supporting you through every stage of your artistic journey. We know that the whole is greater than the sum of its parts.

- **ACTIONABLE INSPIRATION:** We might believe in eating doughnuts as we dabble with paint palettes, but we'll only ever consume (and provide) the type of high-quality creative inspiration that feeds our motivation and fuels our art into action—or *inspir-action*.

- **ENTHUSIASM:** We believe that being creative is a gift. We are so grateful that we can make art—it's pretty darn cool, right? We're unapologetically enthusiastic—and slightly nerdy—about learning and growing as artists.

- **KINDNESS:** We believe that this is a community genuinely and authentically rooted in kindness and compassion. We believe, first and foremost, in being a good human and in taking care of one another through the chaos and craziness of life.

You are officially invited to turn these pillars into something that you are a part of, and dance with us in the messy middle.

HOW TO BE A MESSY ARTIST

If you're still reading, then I haven't scared you away. Maybe I poked at something in the deepest part of your heart. Listen to that something.

This book will teach you how to be a Messy Artist. Every word, written with so much love, is there to encourage you to ignore perfection in lieu of the magic.

The art journal is the means to being a Messy Artist, and we'll show that throughout the book. For now, here's the practical interpretation of the Messy Manifesto:

- **Play in your art journal.**

- **Learn new skills** by practicing techniques that you learn in this book and elsewhere.

- **Make loads of bad art.** Sometimes even on purpose. It will make you a better artist, and it will help you learn that there really is no such thing as bad art. There is just art.

- **Actively ignore perfection.** Treat him like a toddler. Listen to what he says, but don't allow him to drive the car. In fact, let perfection go completely. The sooner you do that, the easier this will be for all of us.

- **Focus on quantity.** It is a much easier way to measure success. Quality will come your way, I promise. Just keep showing up.

- **Be willing to do the work.** Do the work even when you don't feel like it, because that is when you do your best work. Working through the mud and through the nonsense—that's the good stuff. You learn so much.

- **You have big dreams.** I love you for it. But you won't achieve them in a week—if you do, you're not pushing hard enough. What do your dreams look like? If you want a library of journals (that is my dream), then focus on creating just one spread a day. Want to sell your work? Follow the work that sets your heart on fire.

- **Connect with other artists.** You don't have to share every single paint stroke. Figure out what you need from your community and what you can give to it. Create community on your own terms. See chapter 4 for practical ideas and insight into what it can do for your creative life.

- **Give of yourself.** Give advice. Give inspiration. Give wisdom. Give cheerleading. Give kindness.

- **Instead of sitting on Instagram or Pinterest for hours, ask more of yourself.** Leave the house. Go to a coffee shop. Go to a museum. A park. Your back garden or balcony. There is a massive difference in inspiration that is searched for and inspiration that is stumbled upon. Your work will be infinitely different when it comes from deep within, from work done while searching. Are you noticing a theme here? Do. The. Work.

- **Turn inspiration into action.** Inspiration is a raw material and will die without some nurturing.

- **Be grateful for the time you're able to spend creating.** Can you carve out five minutes before falling asleep? If so, you've received five minutes of pure self-love and self-expression and self-creation and self-growth and all of these things wrapped up into one tiny paintbrush!

- **Be grateful that we live in a world that allows us to do this.**

- **Be grateful for every artist that came before you for paving the way.**

- **Remind yourself that there is no place for guilt with art.**

- **Be excited about creating.** The excitement will often be muted but know that this is an inherently exciting thing that we are doing.

- **Be kind in your interactions.**

- **There is a concept in my home country called *ubuntu*.** Remember that we are not alone—we are part of something bigger. When artists are doing well, we are all doing well.

- **The whole is greater than the sum of its parts:** 1 artist + 1 artist doesn't equal 2 artists. It equals something more.

Knowing all of that, let's get into the tangible bit of the Messy Manifesto, the journal.

The Power of the Journal

The art journal is the physical manifestation of the six beliefs of the Messy Artist, providing a tangible medium for you to bring these beliefs into your life. You nurture all those good things in your life by turning to your journal on a regular basis. You also get the bonus of creating a bunch of true art out of your daily life.

There are a bunch more bonuses too, but I won't spoil the surprise.

Art journaling is the thing that takes you from creative dreaming to creative doing. This way of creating brings out the Messy Artist inside of you.

RELEASE YOUR TRUTH, EMOTIONS, AND DREAMS ONTO THE PAGE

When you live in an authentic, imperfect, messy way, you'll automatically be honest in your journal. It is this honesty that will grow art inside of you and enable you to make art that looks the way it does in your head. Over time, you will hone this craft, and your art will look as beautiful as your truth.

There are three truths to know about art journaling: The first page sucks, the middle is a mess, and bad pages are the path to good pages.

The first page sucks

There's no way around it. You may have people around you holding your hand, sharing their knowledge, and making it easier for you, but your first page will never be the Sistine Chapel ceiling on paper. When you let go of that kind of unrealistic expectation, you can create art that is free and true to you. When you're feeling frustrated that things aren't going the way you envisioned, close your eyes, acknowledge that you're doing this for the first time, and move ahead anyway.

The middle is a mess

The messy middle is the part of creation that happens between the excitement of starting and the satisfaction of finishing. It features a whole bunch of imperfection and is sometimes uncomfortable, but it's also the part where you discover the most about yourself and about your art-making process. Making mistakes teaches us so much more than making flawless art ever will.

There's so much excitement that happens the first time, and that can be enough to get you through the beginning. It takes work to extend that excitement, which might make you uncomfortable.

If you feel this discomfort, you've reached the messy middle. Once again, close your eyes, acknowledge it, and move ahead anyway.

If you're unable to tell what moving ahead actually is, then I've got you. I'll tell you. I know a lot about this stuff.

So if the first page sucks and the middle is a mess, then why create art at all?

I have a theory that we're all due a certain number of terrible pages of art before we hit one that we adore. I don't know what that number is, but let's say it's one hundred. Every time you create bad art, rather than beating yourself up about it, just acknowledge that it is one of those designated bad pieces and celebrate the fact that you've checked one off the list. You'll never have to do that one again, and you're closer to that lovely piece.

Shift your focus away from the end result and focus on the process, which is the only thing you have control over.

Knowing that the suckiness and the messiness is part of the journey, and that all artists go through this, makes it more bearable.

The best part about art journaling compared with other art forms is that the imperfections, the suckiness, and the mess are the very best parts. Over time you'll learn this in a deeper way. Over time, you'll find your exact *why* and your art journaling will fulfill this purpose.

I art journal to realign and to let go. Through art journaling, I let go of what's stuck in my head. I process my emotions and articulate my thoughts. I refocus.

Art journaling is deeply personal, and my reason probably won't be your reason. You can see what art journaling is to other artists in the "Connect" chapter near the end.

SO WHAT THE FRIDA KAHLO IS ART JOURNALING?

Art journaling is the practice that takes you from creative dreaming to creative doing. An art journal is a notebook—or a sketchbook, or a piece of paper, or any tool of artistic expression you want—that you fill with drawings, paintings, thoughts, words, lyrics, photos, magazine cut-outs, and ephemera from your life. You're a visual person. Page through this book to see visual representations of art journaling.

Art journals can have lots of words or no words. You can use a journal to document your life and express your emotions, or you can use it to practice art techniques that interest you. Ultimately, art journaling is all about creating for the sake of creating. It's powerful. It's cathartic. It's messy. It's yours.

Or rather—it's ours.

Not a single person inside the Get Messy community has ten uninterrupted hours per day to spend on their art. Art journalers are people with crazy busy lives. They find pockets of time for creating. They schedule a time to create just like doctor appointments. One of our favorite Get Messians, Rose Sheridan (@rosieraindrops, see page 118), takes her art journal with her to the microwave to add a smear of paint as the seconds count down.

I recommend that you decide if you want this in your life. If you do, and you're ready for it, I suggest you make time for it—it will be worth it.

WHY ART JOURNAL?

You'll find reasons to art journal throughout this book, but here are a few quick reasons:

✦ **Art journaling allows you to start from zero.**

The range of expertise for art journalers is wide. Some have a degree in fine art and sell their work in galleries and make marks in a journal, and some are actual children scribbling on paper. You'll fall somewhere in between those two.

You can do it your way. Whatever your zero is, art journaling lets you start from there. Whatever your journey is, art journaling allows it.

✦ **Art journaling helps you grow as an artist.**

You may think, *"I want to be an artist,"* or *"I want to make amazing things."* But then you have no idea what to make, or you think what you make is terrible, or not what you expected. By this point you should know that you're not going to be amazing at something the first time you try it. You must practice, learn, mess up, try again, and then practice some more. As with anything else, practice and repetition are what grow our skills.

Art journaling helps you learn and practice for whatever creative endeavors you want to pursue, allowing you to test the waters and develop your preferences.

✧ Art journaling is self-care.

I love art journaling because it helps me process my thoughts. It helps me understand what I'm feeling before I know I'm feeling it. Art journaling expresses thought and emotion through words and art.

For some of us, journal writing is difficult to maintain. We might be bad at words, or we might feel pressure to write like a professional novelist. But there is so much you can say without words, and art journaling allows you to do it.

✧ Art journaling punches perfection in the face.

Perfectionism is a terrible thing that prevents us from releasing our beauty into the world. The more you art journal, the freer you are in your art because you're not scared of sucking. This "screw perfection" mentality often finds its way into places other than our art journal.

Art journaling is pressure-free messing up. And we totally encourage messing up.

✧ Art journaling creates a huge body of work.

Art journaling gets you from one streak of paint to one page to one finished journal to shelves full of art journals. This body of work serves as a timeline showing how much you've grown as an artist. First art journals are completely different from the latest ones. Working in journals will help you make as much art as possible compared with creating on a canvas or other substrate.

Quality is achieved through quantity. Nothing is better than seeing your finished and unfinished journals piling up on a shelf, knowing that your creative body of work is growing, evolving, and just hanging out in the real world.

✧ **Art journaling is a natural catalyst for consistency and habit.**

Magical things happen when you create consistently. Art journaling helps you be consistently creative when you don't have time to paint a human-sized detailed painting every day. The dedication shown in art journaling regularly will filter into the rest of your life and be glorious.

✧ **Art journaling helps you find your style.**

A large body of work, along with consistent creating, helps you develop your unique style. Spoiler alert: You won't find your style by pinning images with your favorite colors. You'll find your style by showing up and creating every day. Art journaling allows you to use potatoes in your art, discover that you love that, and develop it.

✧ **Art journaling has a lovely community.**

Being part of a community of people who get what you're doing is invaluable. When you're in a slump, they're there to encourage. In the entire history of Get Messy, not once has someone shared their art and received negative feedback—pretty amazing for something that happens online!

Get Messians' least favorite pages often receive the most love. How encouraging to have someone see something you've stared at for too long in a completely different light. Art journalers are on this journey with you. They get you, they get why you're doing this, and they're able to see the beauty.

The Magic of Habit

Were you born with a magical gift, bestowed upon you by the gods, for painting masterpieces on a whim?

Me neither. Talent is just extended periods of hard work. Not one human on this planet was born able to create a masterpiece. A whole bunch of art happens along the way, plus a lot of feeling uncomfortable, not understanding your supplies, not knowing what to do, and straight-up failure.

That shouldn't dishearten you—it should excite you. Hard work means there is a practical way to become the artist you desire to be. Showing up repeatedly is how you turn that hard work into magic.

For me, that habit is doing a little bit every day. For others, it's a once-a-week ritual or creating something on the first day of every month.

In the end, there's no actual magic, just hard work. Or there is magic *and* hard work. And that, my beautiful artist, is called habit. And you get to create it for yourself.

WHAT DOES A CONSISTENT ART PRACTICE LOOK LIKE?

Your art practice will be different from that of all other artists because it fits your life. That practice will also change over time because your life changes.

I used to think that it was vital for an artist to have a daily practice, but I'm no longer certain that the daily practice must involve art supplies. Writing down an idea in your journal or going for a walk around the neighborhood is a creative act. Being creative every day is important—but that creativity can take many different forms.

Here is what a consistent art practice can look like:

- Journaling in bed for five minutes after brushing your teeth

- Waking up half an hour early to spend time creating (see "Tiger Time," page 107)

- Doing something author Julia Cameron calls "morning pages" (three pages of stream-of-consciousness writing) to dump all your thoughts before starting your day

- Taking your art journal to a park bench on your lunch break

- Dropping the kids off at Grandma's house so you can spend Sunday morning creating

- Getting together with a creative group via video chat every Saturday to make and talk about art (see page 114)

Having a habitual practice that fits the current season of your life is more important than having one that's robotlike in its frequency. Habit is just doing the work. Repeatedly.

RITUALS OF CREATING

✦

Rituals can elevate your artistic practice and let your left brain know that it's time to quiet down.

Here are a few small rituals to nurture the magic part of your habit:

- Lighting a candle
- Tying up your hair
- Putting on your paint-stained apron
- Gessoing a page
- Putting your earphones in and listening to music that helps you get in the zone (I'm listening to lo-fi hip-hop right now)
- Putting the kettle on and sitting at your table with a cup of tea
- Cleaning your art space
- Gathering your supplies and following a tutorial
- Scrolling through Instagram (just kidding, there's no way this is conducive to artistic flow)

ANIKA LACERTE

Art as a habit

Anika Lacerte is a Canadian artist who posts her daily drawings on Instagram. In 2016 she started drawing every day with the goal of improving her skills by making a lot of art, and she has completed a dozen successful 100 Day Projects (that's daily creating for one hundred days) without taking a break.

She is the art habit queen. She maintains a sustainable daily art habit by setting the bar low and starting somewhere, then she evaluates, tweaks, and repeats.

Instagram: @thehandcraftedstory

What are your tips for starting a daily art habit?

- **Set the bar low.** My initial goal was to draw for five minutes in a small sketchbook with a black pen before I went to sleep. I was able to maintain this habit because I didn't use a huge variety of supplies and left my supplies out as a reminder. Be realistic about what's happening in your life before setting your daily goals.

- **Start somewhere.** Start with your best guess for the best time of day, length of time, location, supplies, and so on, and then adjust after some time trying it. Decide where you would like to work and prepare your space or make a kit that you can take with you. Attaching your new art habit to an existing habit will help you succeed.

- **Evaluate.** If your initial plan doesn't go as smoothly as expected, evaluate your time or location and make changes so you can keep your art habit going. I have more energy in the mornings, so I adjusted the time of day for my daily habit by setting my alarm to wake up before my kids.

- **Repeat.** Maintaining a daily habit means there will be days when I don't feel like creating. When I lack motivation, it helps to keep a list of ideas, follow art prompts, and break up projects into chunks of time.

- **Be kind to yourself.** When I'm busy, I choose easier themes, and when things are calmer, I challenge myself.

- **Share your project with friends.** Or better yet, recruit your friends to start their own daily projects. Maintaining a daily project is easier if you have encouragement along the way. And don't forget to encourage others, too!

- **Celebrate your work.** Look at past work to see how much you've improved. Use hashtags on social media for projects so you can link them to specific themes within your daily project.

Maintaining a sustainable art habit has allowed me to improve my skills and create a ton of work, and you can do it too.

The Anti-Supply List

Growing up in South Africa, I didn't have a broad range of options for art supplies, and I firmly believe that made me a better artist.

Now that I journal like it's my job—because it is my job—I have more supplies. I don't believe in the starving artist, but I believe that scarcity makes us more creative. See which mediums you like best and make it your goal and challenge to slowly add to your collection.

THE JOURNAL

The journal is the most important supply in art journaling. It's also the one that's the most fun to find.

Your considerations for choosing a journal are size and page count, type of paper, and budget. What you journal in is going to affect the way you create. I'm a very different creator when I'm journaling in a pocket-sized Moleskine Cahier Journal compared with a journal I've bound myself that includes pages made from old books and vintage ledger paper. I make different choices, and I'm drawn to different tools.

If you're new to journaling, my recommendation is to start with a smaller journal with fewer pages.

Heck, that's my recommendation even if you've been journaling for years. Completing a journal gives an immense sense of accomplishment, and if you're working smaller and over fewer pages, you get to feel that more often.

When it comes to paper, one perfect option doesn't exist. Each type of paper comes with its own set of pros and cons. Heavy, luscious watercolor paper can take a lot of water, but it is really thick and it feels clumsy to write on. The beautiful, soft paper included in Tomoe River journals feels like butter against a ballpoint pen, but it will buckle if you use acrylic paint on it.

No matter what type of paper you choose, you can always glue paper on top of it—even with regular printer paper. For example, if you have an inexpensive notebook with paper that's only good for writing, you can paint watercolor onto loose sheets of watercolor paper and adhere that to the paper in your notebook.

If you're exploring mediums, look for mixed media paper. This paper may not meet every need, but it's a jack-of-all-trades. Mixed media paper can handle most things you throw at it—even watercolor, as long as you're light on the water.

You may be restricted by your budget. When I first started journaling, I was a student and would have to work two entire weekends to buy a Moleskine journal at a crazy, imported markup.

When buying a journal, go for something that's "not top of the range," as my dad would say. You don't need the most expensive option, but you deserve something that isn't made for children. Your journal is the place where you can splurge. I give you full permission.

Rather than buying fifty cheap composition books that will make you feel frustrated, buy one good-quality journal, such as one from the Moleskine Art Collection or a Strathmore Mixed Media Art Journal. Fall in love with it. Put your heart and art into it.

Types of journals you'll be choosing from include bound sketchbooks, found books, altered or rebound old books, handbound journals, and zines.

Bound sketchbooks

The easiest way to start journaling is in a bound notebook or sketchbook. They come in an array of sizes, offer various types of papers, and have different page counts.

I recommend going to an art store and feeling a variety of papers. If you enjoy how it feels between your fingers, chances are you'll enjoy creating art on it.

Choose a sketchbook with watercolor paper if that's the medium you want to explore. The paper can accept a lot of water without becoming crinkly or allowing the paint to soak through.

A bound sketchbook cover can be kind of boring, so treat it as you would the inside pages and add your own flavor. Add a sticker or drawing or cover it with wrapping or scrapbook paper and make it yours.

Found books

I always loved collecting the notebooks my dad would bring home from work when I was a teen. As a grown-up, this love has transferred to collecting beautiful pamphlets, catalogs, and booklets. Because I'm an immigrant and I like exploring the idea of heritage, I love working in expired passports.

These found books have terrible paper for creating, which makes me think of creative solutions to how I create in them (see page 38).

Altered or rebound old books

Old books can be repurposed into art journals in two ways: altering a book or rebinding one. Altered books are ones that are worked in while the original pages are still attached. Creating art on the pages of an altered book means that your backgrounds don't have to be plain. Rebound books are created by tearing out the old pages and adding new ones (see page 40). Rebinding a book means that you can put your heart into it, play with different types of paper, and have lots of variety within one journal.

Handbound journals

Handbound journals, ones made completely from scratch, give you all the control—you choose the paper, the size, and the number of pages. A three-hole pamphlet stitch is an easy way to create a simple bound journal, and instructions are easily found online. An even easier process involves punching two holes on the edge of several pieces of paper and connecting them with binder rings or thread. Explore bookmaking so you can create exactly what you need.

Zines

Zines, short for magazines, are typically made from one sheet of paper that's been folded to create a booklet. This is the easiest way to make a small, six-page journal for creating art.

STARTER ART JOURNAL KIT

I understand wanting to buy all the supplies before starting—that's a human characteristic. I also understand wanting to make sure the conditions are perfect before taking that leap of faith and jumping in. But you'll never get those perfect conditions, and it's far easier, better, more fulfilling, and just plain fun to embrace the mess.

Buying countless supplies outsources creativity while having fewer tools forces you to be more creative—which is the entire point.

If you want to start art journaling today, this is the kit I recommend you assemble:

- **A great pen for writing, doodling, and making marks:** My favorite is the Pilot G2 because it feels like you're gliding on paper.

- **A brush pen:** Kuretake brush pens are perfect for blind contour drawing and loose lettering. They enable me to loosen up because I have less control with them than a regular pen. They behave like a paintbrush dipped into ink with the added benefit of having the ink flow through the nib instead of having to continually dip the brush.

- **A few tubes of acrylic craft paint:** Some brands can be found for less than $1 per bottle. (At one point I forced my husband to bring fifty back home for me from the U.S.)

- **A palette:** You don't need a formal one; you can use an old plate (I love my nana's chipped, gold-rimmed cake plates) or even a sheet of paper for paint mixing.

- **A small set of pan watercolors:** Watercolors (and other types of paint) come in grades, such as student and professional. If your budget allows, go for the student grade (try Winsor & Newton or Schmincke brands). Handmade watercolor is readily available on Etsy; these tend to be expensive, so buy half-pans (each holds about 2 ml of paint) individually as you build up your color selection.

- **Three inexpensive paintbrushes** (grab a mix of round and flat): One large, one medium, and one small

- **An expired credit or gift card** for applying paint

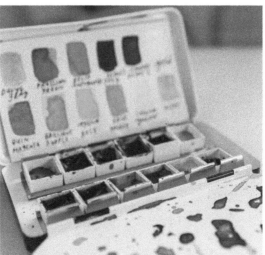
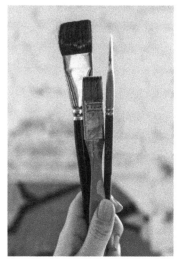

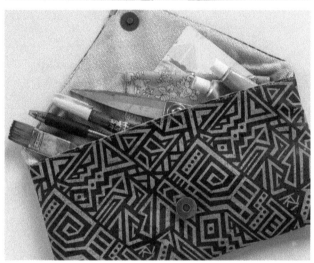

- **Stencil designs** that you're drawn to

- **Found papers:** Old magazines and books are good for images. You can also find copyright-free images online, and Etsy is a good place to find packs of ephemera.

- **Personal papers and images:** I'm a magpie and I collect paper (pamphlets, notes to myself, envelopes) and photos (passport and photobooth photos are favorites). I believe in including photos of yourself in your journals.

- **A large, sturdy clip** to hold your journal open while working in it, or to keep a pile of ephemera together

- **A glue stick** for collage

- A sharp pair of **scissors**

- **A small box or pencil case** to house everything

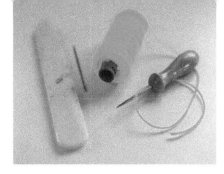

Once you've invested time in this hobby and enjoy it, level up with the following (in order):

- **Gesso (pronounced jesso):** Gesso is an acrylic medium that is often used to prime a surface. It can be mixed with other acrylics. It comes in white, clear, black, and colors.

- **Matte medium:** Matte medium is loved as a wet glue in collage because it dries clear. It can also be added to acrylic paint to give a matte finish. This medium can be tacky when dry, so add a sheet of wax paper between your journal pages or rub a small amount of talcum powder on top of your pages to prevent them from sticking together.

- **Modeling paste:** This bad boy acrylic medium is my favorite because it feels like thick cake frosting. Pair it with a stencil to create an image that has dimension or mix it with acrylic paint to add texture. This is an essential supply for me since it's an easy way to add texture and dimension.

- **Tape runner:** This dry glue dispenses a line of adhesive and allows you to attach almost any papers without warping.

- **Paint markers or pens:** Uni-POSCA markers have the best quality that I've found—they feel like acrylic but are actually pigment paint.

- **Higher-quality acrylic paint:** I love Golden Heavy Body Acrylic paints because they feel like smearing butter on the page. They're thick and will leave luscious brushstrokes once dry. Golden High Flow Acrylic has a heavy, creamlike consistency that's perfect for more fluid painting.

- **Higher-quality watercolor paints:** Tube paints are an alternative to pan watercolors and are more versatile. They're perfect for painting larger areas and will give you a more vibrant color. My favorite brands are Winsor & Newton and Schmincke.

- **A good-quality watercolor paintbrush:** My favorite type of brush is a mop brush made from squirrel hair because it allows you to pick up a lot of water. To upgrade more of your brushes, Winsor & Newton's Cotman brushes are wonderful; try an angled tip for washes and a Winsor & Newton Series 7 Kolinsky Sable Brush, size 1, for fine lines.

- **A great paint palette:** One of my palettes has sprinkles embedded in it, and it always cheers me up.

- **A silicone brush:** These glide over paper and allow you to create a thin film of paint.

- **Acrylic ink:** Make splatters on your artwork with a paintbrush loaded with ink and water. Acrylic inks usually come with droppers, and those are fun to use for drawings and mark-making as well.

- **Thread:** I like incorporating fibers into my journals by hand sewing embroidery thread and running paper through my sewing machine. This is a great way to add color, texture, and pattern to your pages.

- **Bookbinding supplies:** The basics include a needle and thread, an awl, and a bone folder (see page 44 for more ideas).

- **Typewriter or computer:** These can be used for printing out journaling in interesting typefaces.

- **Metal palette knife:** This tool is a great way to mix paint.

- **Gold metallic flakes:** These add shine, and they'll make a mess, but you'll have fun trying to keep them under control.

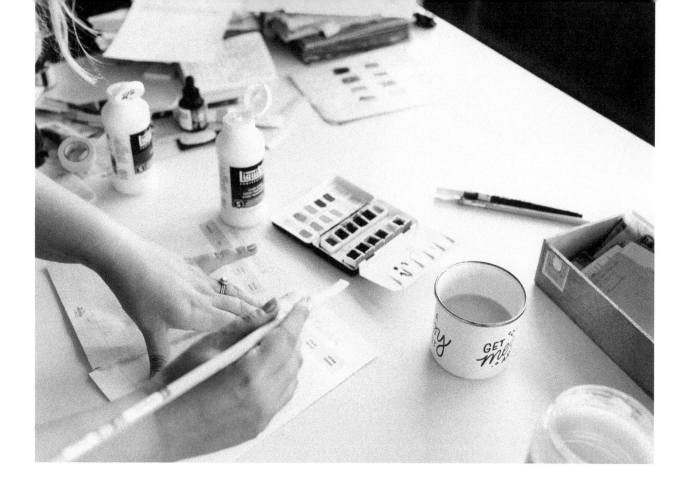

FALL IN LOVE WITH WHAT YOU HAVE

A lot of pleasure comes from trying out new supplies and discovering the way they feel and the type of marks they make. Going crazy with new supplies is easy, but there is something to be said for slowly, thoughtfully making your way through the ones you already have. Take some time to learn about and explore each medium. Watch YouTube videos, search online, ask your favorite artists about them, and watch how others use supplies. Play. By doing all this and honing in on a select few, your confidence will grow.

I believe that we expand our creativity by setting limits, and that's the main reason why I love minimalism. We're overwhelmed and don't know where to start when we have too many supplies. We create more with only a few supplies because we love using them. Our style emerges and we become prolific.

Put aside some time for complete play to see which mediums you like. Make it your motto, goal, mantra, and challenge to add to your collection slowly.

A NOTE ABOUT COLOR

When it comes to choosing colors to work with, I recommend that you choose your favorite shades. If you're interested in learning color theory, you can start with a few basics and experiment with mixing them, but I prefer selecting what I'm drawn to. Don't worry if the colors match or if you have all the colors you need.

SWATCHING

Swatching, or recording small samples of your art supplies, is one of my favorite creative practices. The activity requires low effort (which I love because I'm lazy), and it's easy (because I create art for fun, not as a chore). The technique is also super satisfying.

Swatching will help you fall in love with your supplies. Let's get our supplies on.

Things to swatch:

- Your favorite supplies

- A watercolor palette

- A set of paints

- A medium layered over white, clear, or other types of gesso (not all gesso is created equal)

- A medium layered over another medium

- Different colors of the same brand of supply

- Different brands of the same color

- Mediums on different papers (this is a favorite of mine)

- Mediums applied with different tools (paintbrushes, fingers, a stick, a carved potato, etc.)

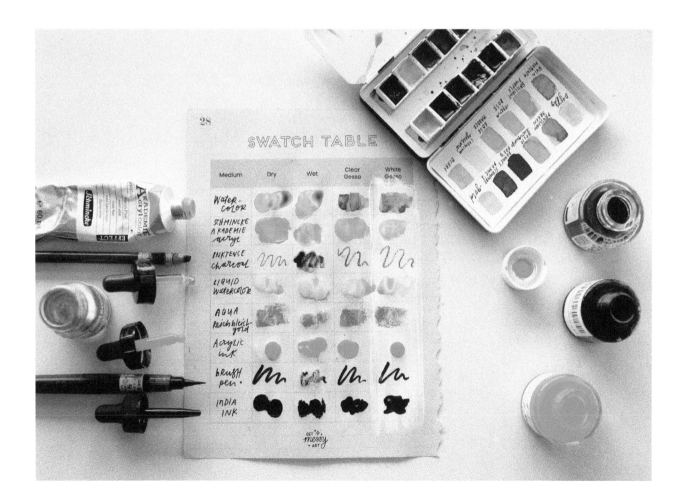

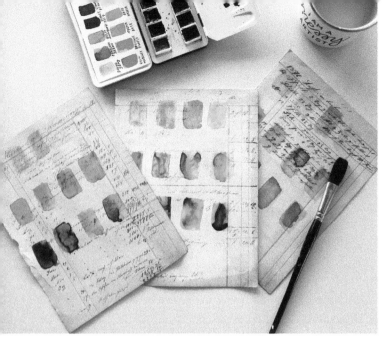

Exercise: Simple supply swatches

This exercise will guide you in testing a supply in an intentional way.

Grab a sheet of paper and go wild. See how your paint reacts on a variety of papers, including found papers, such as ledger and book pages. Prepare the papers in different ways to see what effect each ground has on various mediums.

I used three vintage ledger papers, each prepared a different way: one with white gesso, one with clear gesso, and one plain. I like creating grid swatches, but you might prefer blobs all over the page, making splashes, or creating a color wheel.

Seeing the page burst into color is such a delight, and the results are even better when there are no expectations. This is pure play—I'm not trying to make art, I'm just putting color on the page.

TIPS FOR SWATCHING

Swatches don't have to be purely functional—you can use them in your art as well.

Get Messian Sarah Rondon (Instagram: @sjrondon) made a swatch book after she brought home too many watercolor paints in colors she already had. She takes the book with her to the art supply store and checks colors against her swatches. Sometimes she tries out new supplies to see what they look like with her collection.

Here are some tips for working with swatches:

- Keep the scrap paper you use when you swatch colors for a painting.
- Color names can be whimsical and fun to include.
- Getting together with friends and swatching their collections is a great way to try different supplies. I swatched these paints while meeting up with artist friends. ▶
- Colors aren't the only things to swatch—you can include papers, too.

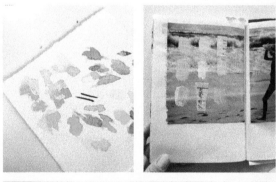

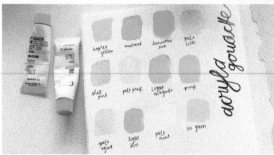

Exercise: Swatch tables

When I feel particularly fancy, I'll print out a swatch table, available as a resource under getmessyart.com/bookclub. Swatch tables allow you to try different mediums on a variety of papers and make notes about the results so you have a record of your experiments. If you're using a wet medium, print the swatch table using a laser printer so the ink doesn't smear. I printed mine onto two types of heavy watercolor paper and vintage ledger paper. If you don't have a laser printer, draw the grid by hand.

1. Choose a medium or mediums and a variety of substrates. I started with a watercolor palette paired with dry paper, wet paper, and paper coated with clear and white gesso. Make sure to note the medium you're working with on the substrate.

2. Take your time experimenting with each supply, seeing how it reacts to plain paper, water, and gesso.

3. Make a note of your favorite tests for the next time you work in your art journal. These swatches provide a clear list of options if you're ever short of ideas.

Creating Your Messy Journal

CHANGE YOUR ART JOURNALING GAME BY BINDING YOUR OWN JOURNALS

One thing will change the art journaling game for blossoming beginners and prolific pros alike: binding your own journal.

Bookbinding, though, can be exceptionally difficult, and I'm exceptionally lazy—or exceptionally efficient, depending on your perspective.

Enter the *junk journal*, a handmade book with a terrible name and a wonderful personality. The earliest junk journals were made by binding up the paper junk of everyday life—such as spam mail, bills, old calendars, and big envelopes—into a journal used for creating. Nowadays, junk journals are anything but junk. They're works of art.

This particular way of binding a junk journal is a very easy step-by-step technique. It requires only imperfect action that, by default, delights in the messy middle and actively ignores perfection.

You're welcome to use your junk and your treasures to make this journal, and to bind it imperfectly. You'll find that even old receipts and ticket stubs can become art.

Binding your own journal helps the creative process because you're not starting from zero. Creating is easier when you're responding to something. A handbound journal, with pages you've chosen, gives you that base.

I prefer using paper that I've collected for a special occasion. The journal is my special occasion. I use vintage papers, my son's artwork, scraps leftover from trying a new technique, old letters and cards, and anything else that draws me in and is about the size of a journal page.

I like things in a particular way, with perfect little marks all lined up, so I could spend hours perfecting my binding techniques. But I don't have that time, and I do have an affinity for messiness.

With this technique you don't have to worry about paper grain, or which way to fold, or using special thread—you'll figure things out as you go.

Note: In addition to the supplies you need to make your journal, I've also included optional level-up items that boost the kick-assery of the project.

materials

- An old book (Choose a book with a sturdy spine. It should be old and beautifully worn, but not falling apart.)
- Craft knife
- Decorative paper for lining the inside of the book (optional)
- Glue: I use a glue tape, but you could also use PVA adhesive (choose pH neutral so that it won't yellow over time).
- Scrap paper for spine and page templates
- Selection of papers for the inside pages (see "Paper Chase" sidebar) (level up: choose a color palette)
- Ruler or straightedge for folding paper (level up: a bonefolder makes neat creases and will make your bookbinding life easier)
- Pencil
- Low-tack removable tape
- Thin bookbinding awl (level up: Japanese screw punch with a small tip; this will make clean holes in the spine)
- Binding clip
- Embroidery thread (level up: 4-ply waxed linen bookbinding thread)
- Beeswax
- Needle (level up: choose a needle with an eye large enough to accommodate the thread, but not so large that it struggles going through the pages and spine)
- Optional items for decorating the cover: metal book corners, labels, lace trim, eyelet and snap punches

Prepare the Cover

1. Loosen the book's spine by opening it up and bending the covers back a bit.

2. Pull the book's *text block* (group of pages) away from the cover; this should reveal the gap between the text block and the cover, which is the easiest place to cut.

3. Cut the text block from the spine on one side, using a craft knife. Slide the tip of the knife along the gap between the text block and spine, making sure the knife doesn't pierce the spine. If you do pierce it, you can reinforce the spine later with duct tape.

4. Pull the cover away from the pages.

5. Repeat on the other side, which should be much easier to cut and separate.

6. Once the cover has been separated from the pages, you can leave it as is, since you'll be sewing into the spine, or you can line the inside cover. I glued decorative wrapping paper to the inside using a tape runner. When gluing, hold the book semi-closed so that you cover the entire surface and the paper doesn't tear.

Create the pages

I'm terrible at measuring things, but feel free to measure if you'd like. To cut down on measuring, I grab a piece of paper, fold it in half, cut it slightly smaller than the book, and use that as a template to guide me for the pages. Creating simple templates allows you to be loose and imperfect and messy and figure things out as you go along.

1. Create one template for the spine and one for the pages. Measure the height and width of the spine and cut a piece of scrap paper to these measurements.

2. To create a template for the pages, fold a piece of scrap paper in half; it should be larger than the journal. Place the folded edge against the spine and cut it to fit. The folded paper should be slightly shorter than the cover at the top and bottom and about ¼" (0.5 cm) shorter on the open side, also called the fore edge. If you have the original pages from the book, you can use them as size guides for the journal pages.

3. Choose the papers for the book and fold them to form the pages. Create a variety of page sizes to add interest. Be ruthless in deciding what to keep—just because you folded it doesn't mean it has to stay. Be aware of how the pages look next to each other.

Nest several folded pages together, one inside the other; this is called a signature. Decide how many signatures you'd like in the book (for this binding, you'll need multiples of two). The number of signatures will depend on the width of the spine and the number and thickness of the pages. A signature typically includes four to five pages folded, or eight to ten pages total.

Keep in mind that nesting pages together to form a signature pushes the front edges (also called the fore edges) out, so you may need to trim the signatures to fit.

4. Once your signatures are complete, put them between the covers with the folded edges against the spine, and see how they fit. Is the cover sagging? Add more paper to your signatures or add extra signatures. Bursting at the seams? Remove some of your least favorite pages or remove signatures. My book has a 1" (3 cm) spine, so I created two signatures.

5. Create a spine template without measuring by folding the spine template paper in half vertically to find the midpoint. Fold each half in half again vertically, creating four sections. Create the same folds horizontally by folding the paper in half horizontally, then folding each half in half once again.

You should have three folds across vertically and five horizontally.

6. Draw a small dot where the folds intersect. Attach the template to the outside of the spine using low-tack, removable tape (I used washi tape).

7. Using the spine template as a guide, punch a hole through the spine at each mark with a thin awl or a small bit bookbinding punch (also called a Japanese screw punch).

8. Remove the spine template from the book. Place the folded edge of the page template along one row of holes on the spine template and make sure the edges are even (there will probably be some overhang at the top and bottom). Make a mark on the fold at each dot on the spine template. Fold the page template the other way, so the marks are on the inside.

9. Place the template in the middle of one signature and punch holes through the template and signature at each mark using a thin awl. Wiggle the awl around to widen the hole. Wider holes make for easy binding.

If the pages shift while you're punching holes, use a sturdy binding clip to hold them together.

Let's bind, baby

Take a deep breath—we're going to put this all together.

Note: This binding involves sewing two signatures at the same time into the cover. When you go out of one signature and into another, always go through the cover and the signature. If you have another pair of signatures, finish one set first, then do the second set.

1. Cut a piece of thread that's about six times the length of your book—I prefer working with too much thread than too little. If using embroidery thread, run it along a piece of beeswax for the ultimate smooth, knot-free experience before threading the needle.

Note: Use the diagram as a guide. Once you've bound your first Messy Journal, binding others will become intuitive and you'll understand the process better.

1A 1B

2A 2B

3A 3B

4A 4B

5A 5B

2. Start with the second signature (the one facing the back cover). Enter through hole 1A from the inside, leaving a 3" (7.5 cm) thread tail. Enter hole 2B from the outside. You're now inside the first signature.

3. Travel up the signature and enter hole 1B from the inside. Enter hole 2A from the outside. You're now back inside of the second signature.

BINDING TIPS

- Keep the thread taut by always pulling parallel to the spine in the direction you're sewing—never pull straight up. Tight threads improve the book's structural integrity and the look of the double-X binding pattern.
- If you're struggling to go through both the spine hole and the signature, separate the two a bit and go through the hole first and then the signature.
- Feel your way around. Figure things out. Keep trying.
- For an elevated look, you can bind the journal with two colors of thread by simply putting both into the eye of your needle. This will make your thread thicker and less nimble, so only try this once you've bound a few books.

4. Travel down the signature and enter hole 3A from the inside. Enter hole 4B from the outside. Enter hole 3B from the inside and enter hole 4A from the outside. You should now have two X stitches on the outside of the spine.

5. Enter hole 5A from the inside, enter hole 4B from the outside, enter hole 5B from the inside, and enter hole 4A from the outside, completing another X on the spine.

6. Make the final X on the spine. Travel up the second signature and enter hole 3A from the inside. Enter hole 2B from the outside, enter hole 3B from the inside, and enter hole 2A from the outside.

    Tie the tail thread and the working thread in a tight knot and trim the threads to ½" (1 cm).

7. Your journal is now complete! Marvel at your creation.

This X stitch is my favorite way of binding. You can create journals using other easy binding methods, easily found in books and online. Here are the spines of some of my other handmade journals.

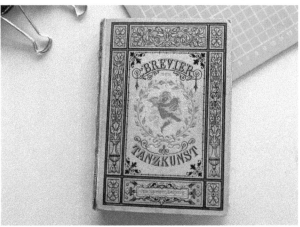

ARTISTIC
DESERT

IDEA BRIDGE

SPARK

JOURNEY GUIDE

SPARK TRAIL
GROW TRAIL
CULTIVATE TRAIL

BLOSSOMING BEGINNER FIELDS

SPORADIC RD

EXPERIMENT LANE

PERFECTIONISM
SWAMP

GROW

MESSY MIDDLE TRAIL

NEW ADVENTURE RD

CULTIVATE

PROLIFIC PRO

PASS

OFF TRACK

ARTISTIC FREEDOM

BEACH

THE
TRAILS

· ·

This book is a map for your creativity. But this isn't a normal map because you're not a normal human. Creativity isn't something that begins at one point and ends at another. It would be far easier if it were, but you'd miss out on the beauty of the messy middle.

This book features a trio of trails, plus one extra. You can (and are encouraged to) explore each trail multiple times, wandering through each section in order or roaming them like hiking trails. The creative journey is a messy one, and you'll need different tools at different stages.

You'll benefit from the techniques and ideas in the first trail as much as the others, whether you're just beginning to think about art or you've been creating for decades. No trail is better than the others—just different.

Each trail represents a different part of the Messy Artist's journey: "Spark," "Grow," and "Cultivate," make up the trio, and "Connect" holds them together. Think of this fourth bonus trail as a level up to whatever trail you're on.

The goal is to go from artistic desert to artistic freedom. To create art. The keys to creating art involve acting on your ideas—ignoring, embracing, and creating despite yearning for perfection—and making a lot of art: good, bad, terrible, hilarious, true. All of it.

Between these trails are a few minor trails linking back and forth between sections. These are the trails you'll take on your own, inspired by, but not led by this book. You can experiment, try new adventures, or lose your way altogether. Losing your way and finding it back is where the magic happens.

SPARK

SPARK YOUR CREATIVITY AND LAUNCH YOUR ART JOURNALING HABIT

Sometimes we need someone to tell us exactly what to do and to be as exact as a math equation.

This trail requires absolutely zero creative inspiration and ignores flow, rendering motivation unnecessary.

Show up as you are and with the supplies you have. This is the practical trail with the lowest barrier to entry. This trail is perfect if you're just getting started in art or returning to it after a long hiatus.

You might be in need of this trail because you're feeling creatively drained. You may feel as though you are an arid desert, artistically dry. Over the following pages you'll find new ways to find that creative oasis and begin creating again.

project MESSY RECIPES

materials

- Low-tack, removable tape
- Acrylic paint
- Repurposed gift or credit card
- Ephemera
- Typewriter or writing instrument, such as a ballpoint pen or acrylic paint pen
- Sewing machine or needle and thread
- Flowers
- Photo of yourself or a magazine photo
- Scissors
- Washi tape, stitching, or patterned paper
- Book page
- Stencil
- Palette knife
- Modeling paste or white acrylic paint

Think of a Messy Recipe like cooking: I'll give you the steps and you make the cake. You're free to be as liberal or precise with this recipe as you'd like.

The best part about art recipes is that you can follow them a million times and have different results each time. They prevent you from thinking too much and allow you to just have fun with your art.

Recipe 1: Thread together

1. Choose a double page spread in your journal and portion out a little more than half; you will paint this section later. Use a strip of low-tack, removable tape to create a clean line on one page.

2. Paint the pages with a solid color of acrylic paint using an old gift or credit card to apply the paint in a thin layer. Remove the tape.

3. Select a few pieces of ephemera that speak to you and complement the color you chose for the background paint.

4. Use a typewriter or handwrite your favorite song lyrics on one of the pieces of ephemera. If a regular ballpoint pen won't write easily on your ephemera, an acrylic paint pen usually will. Attach the bits of paper to your journal with hand or machine stitching using contrasting colored thread.

Recipe 2: You deserve flowers

1. Buy yourself a bouquet of flowers! Yes, this is a step and I'm giving you an excuse to buy flowers.

2. Choose three of your favorite flowers and create a blind contour drawing (see page 82).

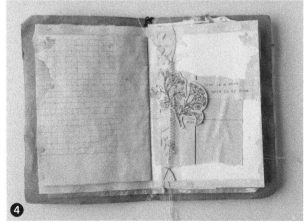

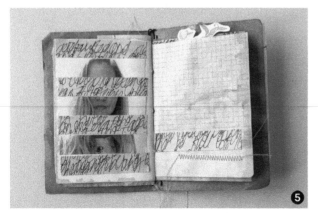

Recipe 3: Pieces of me

1. Paint a sheet of paper in a solid color. Write your thoughts on it. Use loose, messy writing, and let it flow in a stream of consciousness. How are you feeling? What is your current mood? What is the season of life that you're going through? What's on your mind? What do you need more of? What do you need less of? Keep writing until the page is full. Write more on top of that until your writing is illegible and you have nothing more to say.

2. Take a photo of yourself after you have unloaded everything and print it. If you don't have a printer, use an old photo of yourself or an image from a magazine that represents how you feel.

3. Cut the photo and the handwritten page into strips.

4. Alternate the strips and adhere them to one page, leaving one written strip for the other side.

5. Add a strip of color with washi tape, stitching, or patterned paper to finish off the spread.

Recipe 4: Whiteout poetry

1. Select a page from a book written in a language you understand.

2. Choose words from the page that you're drawn to. Brush white acrylic paint onto the page, leaving the words you've selected unpainted. The words don't have to form a sentence, but they can if you'd like.

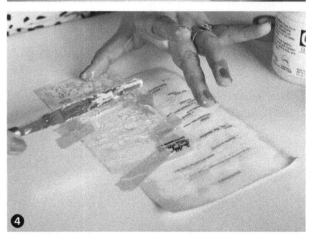

3. Adhere a stencil to the page using low-tack removable tape.

4. Apply modeling paste through the stencil using a palette knife to stencil a design on top of the page.

Messy Recipes take away your control; less thinking means more room for creativity.

This lesson offers several opportunities to spark your creativity if you:

- Would like to level up from your previous recipe or project

- Are feeling creatively dry

- Are looking for self-created guidance

- Would like to explore your supplies

- Would like to experiment with a technique you've been meaning to try for ages

- Need self-imposed structure to your creativity

- Would like to leave your creativity up to chance (ooh!)

You get to choose the ingredients for this recipe. You'll use a die to leave things up to chance, which means even less control.

1. Write three categories of creative influences on a piece of paper. These can be as straightforward as a medium or technique, or as abstract as an artistic influence. I chose a medium, a color (regardless of medium), and a technique.

❶

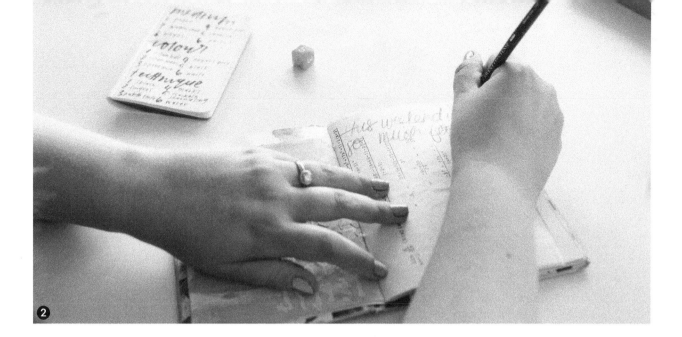

Under each category, write down six of your favorite subcategories. My mediums were paper, watercolor, acrylic paint, a brush pen, charcoal, and oil paste. My colors were titan buff, titan mars pale, opera rose, Payne's grey, black, and white. My techniques were splash, using my fingers, using a palette knife, mark-making, scribble journaling, and incorporating water. Always create using your favorites.

2. Roll a die three times to get your recipe. The first roll comes from your first category, second roll from your second category, and so on. Using my list as an example, if the numbers are two, five, and seven, combine the second item on the mediums list with the fifth item on the colors list and the seventh item on the techniques list.

If your creative well is dry and you're still unsure about what to do, just keep rolling to get more specifics about what to create next. You're also welcome to roll fewer times; my paper medium, for example, might not need a technique since I know what to do with it.

MORE CATEGORY IDEAS

- **Simple marks:** dots, circles, plus signs, hearts, etc.
- **Lettering:** brush script, block letters, cursive, typewritten, hand-sewn, nondominant hand lettering
- **Writing (yours or your favorite writer's):** poetry, song lyrics, a favorite quote (see page 64)
- **Media:** podcast episode, audiobook, vlog, playlist that you enjoy listening to while you create
- **Imagery:** floral motif, self-portrait, architecture, symbols, favorite animal, sweets
- **Pressure on the page:** hard, soft, uneven, loose, controlled, skirting across the page
- **Artist influence:** famous artists, art journalers from this book, favorite online creators
- **Broad theme:** adventure, love, truth, freedom, growth, story
- **Tutorial:** sourced online or from a book, video, or workshop
- **Lesson from this book:** choose six at random, assigning a number to each one

Categories don't need to be perfectly aligned. This game is meant as a guide, so if things don't quite fit, just be more creative.

3. Here's what my die told me: I rolled a six, which meant charcoal as a medium, so I could ignore the color roll. I rolled a five for technique, so I'd start my page with scribble journaling. Scribble journaling is writing whatever comes to mind loosely. The point of scribble journaling is just to get your thoughts out—you don't need to make beauty.

4. To level up the journaling, I rolled again for a technique, which allowed me to add water to the scribbling—this produced a great blurring effect in my journaling.

5. I rolled the die three times, and the numbers indicated a watercolor splash with Payne's grey. I dipped my brush into water, then onto the watercolor pigment and back into the water, making a splash by loosely plopping my brush onto the page.

6. Once the watercolor was dry, I rolled the die again; I'd be using titan mars pale acrylic paint with my fingers. I smeared it around.

   I loved that acrylic so much that I rolled for another technique and got mark-making. I knew I wanted to make marks with my flat brush, so I grabbed a bit of paint and used the tip to create random rectangular shapes.

7. Another roll directed me to play with watercolor (opera rose) and make splashes. I used a different splashing technique this time: I loaded my brush with color and water, held the brush high, and dropped the bright pink onto the page.

   See page 54 for the completed page. I'll bet that if you use the same materials and techniques, you won't end up with what I did. Even if I played this game again and rolled all the same numbers in the same order, I wouldn't either.

   Consider these pages finished or use them as a base for deciding what to do next without the die.

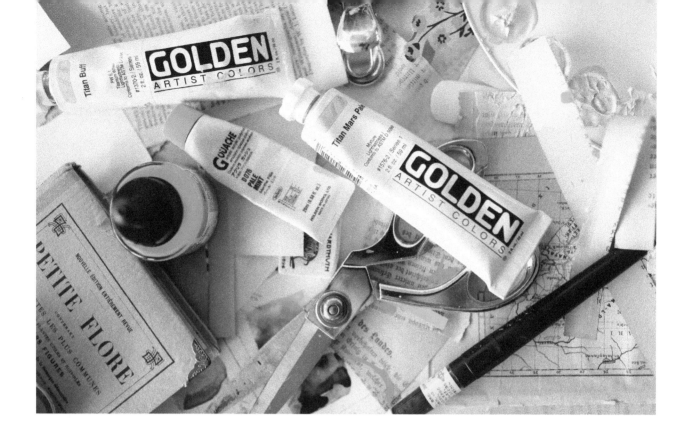

PROMPTS

Prompts are a guiding light while creating. A prompt offers a suggestion for what to create but leaves enough interpretation for your creativity to shine. We believe prompts are the key to:

- Giving you something to art journal about when your mind is blank

- Pushing your journaling to the next level and expressing deeper meaning in your art

- Challenging you to explore new techniques

- Sparking more ideas

- Breaking a creative rut

All this awesomeness is why we share prompts consistently in the Get Messy community, and why I've included a set of prompts for you.

How to respond to a prompt

Prompts are not rules; they're a starting point, a catalyst. Take what you need from them and discard the rest. Prompts are a call to action. By deciding that a prompt isn't for you, you're showing you're ready to create. The hard part is done—simply find a prompt that speaks to you and dive in.

Some of my favorite prompts

My favorite go-to prompts are below—and throughout the book—but you can also make your own. If a new idea for a prompt comes to you while doing the wash, while creating, while reading this book, write it down and revisit it.

- What is your journal a home for?

- What does "fail flamboyantly" mean to you?

- What makes up who you are?

- Create a self-portrait in objects. What is this collection of you?

- What nice thing has someone said to you?

- Write in the third person.

- Write a letter to yourself. At the top write, "Dear (name)," and give yourself what you need.

- What have you learned to love?

- What is your one golden rule for being an artist?

- Write a permission slip.

- Write out the Messy Manifesto. What would you add?

- Choose a project in this book and do it with a different medium.

- Scroll through the #getmessybook or #getmessyartjournal on Instagram. Use one of those projects as a recipe for creating. Be sure not to copy artwork outright. Share and tag the artist.

② GROW

GROW AS AN ARTIST BY EXPANDING YOUR KNOWLEDGE AND SKILLS

You can grow your creativity in depth or breadth. While depth takes time and patience to achieve, expanding your breadth of knowledge can happen in fifteen minutes. Learning new ways of doing things from other artists gives you a host of ideas.

When you mix your creative magic with another artist's creative magic through learning from them, the only thing you can expect is to grow.

For the "Grow" trail I've enlisted the help of some of my favorite wildly creative artists who share their art and their heart with you. I'll also be sharing several of my favorite go-to techniques, including easy color-mixing methods, illustrating, and working with modeling paste and stencils. All these lessons will take you out of your comfort zone, but that's where the best stuff happens. So don't be afraid—you have us to hold your hand.

project ADDING COLOR WITHOUT KNOWING THE DIFFERENCE BETWEEN TINTS AND HUES

This is an easy technique if you would love to play with color but have zero technical know-how—you just need your favorite shades of paint.

materials

- Black and white image that fits inside your journal
- Acrylic paint or Acryla gouache, four favorite colors
- Paintbrushes, size 10 filbert brush (bristles should be about ½" (1 cm) wide), and a small, thin brush
- India ink

1. Adhere a black and white image to the middle of a journal page. Choose four favorite colors of paint; I chose Acryla gouache, but you could use acrylic paint. Create loose triangles of color on two opposite corners of the image, using a paintbrush or your fingertip. I used a size 10 filbert brush, with bristles about ½" (1 cm) wide. Leave the center free.

2. Add a second layer of dots semi-randomly in another color, making sure to fill in some of the gaps between the previous dots.

3. Add a third color of paint, using the same techniques. Extend the dots onto the opposite page.

4. Add the fourth color; by this time, any open spaces will be obvious. Fill them with dots of paint. I love this technique because it allows you to play with colors without overthinking it. The end result is harmonious, and you'll quickly become more comfortable working with color.

Play with the size and placement of the paint dots. Here I've used them around a central image. Instead of acrylic paint, try watercolor and let the edges bleed together.

5. Dip a thin paintbrush into black India ink and letter a favorite quote or saying. I wrote *vive ut vivas*, which means "live life to the fullest."

HAVE FUN WITH PEN AND BRUSH LETTERING

Don't worry about creating perfect calligraphy. I find that messy, imperfect lettering has far more character. Here are some ideas to try:

- Use a variety of pens, brushes, and mediums.
- Hold your pen loosely.
- Hold your pen differently from how you usually hold one.
- Write at a slant.
- Make your lines thick on the downstrokes.
- Apply different levels of pressure as you write.
- Mix uppercase and lowercase letters.
- Mix script and print.
- Go over your letters again after you've written them.
- Make art out of the magic of the uppercase R (or any other letter that calls to you).

- Change the position of a letter.
- Write loosely.
- Condense the letters as you write.
- Bounce the letters.
- Listen to music while writing.
- Write on smooth paper, watercolor paper, or over gritty gesso.
- Let your mood influence your writing.
- Write quickly.
- Write slowly.
- Acknowledge your feelings and allow them to influence your lettering.

ASHLEY RODGERS

Express more with less

Ashley Rodgers is an artist with a bachelor's degree in art history from the University of Virginia. Her art journals represent an introspective process. With few materials and a limited color palette she has developed a minimal, yet expressive style rooted in love, light, and hope, and her goal is to move and inspire others through her work.

Instagram: @sweetashleyann

I believe less is more. This project is an easy four-step process that allows you to transfer your thoughts and feelings onto the page and find inner peace and calm.

There is beauty in simplicity. Simplifying a deep, introspective process is a delicate balance, but the result is truly satisfying. The artwork is aesthetically pleasing and draws viewers in, inviting them to pause and examine their own thoughts and feelings.

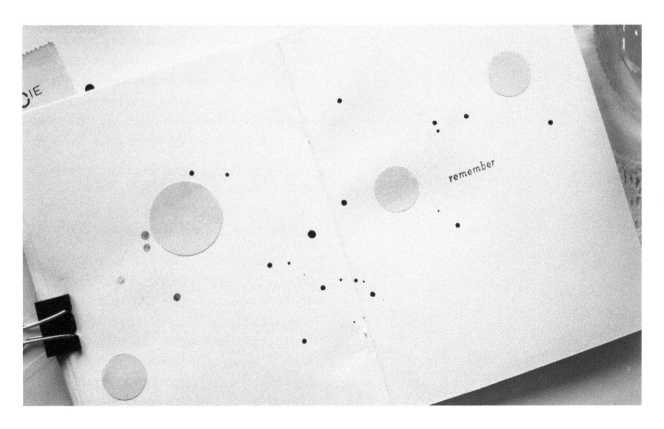

materials

- Paper and ephemera scraps
- Acrylic paint
- Small, round paintbrush
- Palette
- Paper punch

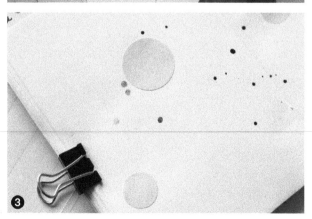

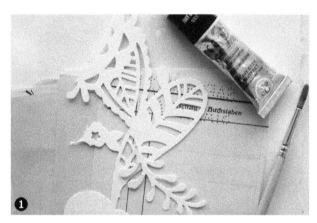

1. Choose a limited color palette. I use three to four colors when creating a work of art: usually black, white, and an accent color. Black and white adds high contrast, and using one accent color creates enough interest to engage the viewer without overstimulating the eye. Because I love mixed-media collage, I gathered some vintage papers, a few paper scraps, and black acrylic paint.

2. Embrace the blank page. I love white space because it's crisp and clean and feels light when I'm dealing with heavy emotions. A blank page can be intimidating, but think of it as an open invitation to express yourself with no pressure or judgment. Take a deep breath. This is the time to pause and reflect. Articulate your feelings in a meaningful way with intention and purpose.

3. Create a sense of movement. Movement is a key principle of art and can be achieved multiple ways through line, color, and shape. I like to splatter paint. This technique often represents scattered thoughts or feelings of chaos or discomfort because the outcome is less controlled. I used a small round brush to create a few small paint splatters. Just saturate the brush with paint and water and lightly tap on it to distribute paint across the page.

4. Punch some shapes out of scrap paper and adhere them to the page. I punched various sizes of circles in pink. This makes the page more dynamic and helps carry the eye around the page.

5. Add a focal point. The focal point is the main focus of the composition and brings order back to the page. When placed thoughtfully, it draws the viewer in and provides a resting place for the eye. Here, I added one simple word as the focal point. Notice how your attention is drawn to that one word even though it's the smallest element in the composition (see finished artwork on page 65).

FELICITAS MAYER

Messy watercolors and abstract florals

Note from Caylee: Create texture and play with watercolors and other mediums in this messy technique. Explore color, abstract shapes, and florals, and bring them together to create a visual representation of your mind.

Felicitas Mayer is a product designer who has been in the memory-keeping industry for ten years. While she documents her life story with photos and papers for a living, she finds joy and relaxation in art journaling and all things mixed media.

Instagram: @felicitasmayer

When I created this page, I was busy with all kinds of things and I wanted to express that creatively. Here is how I made my busy mind visible.

materials

- Deli paper sheets
- Paintbrushes
- Matte medium
- Gesso or white acrylic paint
- Acrylic paints, various colors
- Acrylic marker
- Black and white self-portrait photo
- Watercolor
- Waterproof fine line pen, black

1. Gather supplies and materials—I love to combine different mediums like gesso, matte medium, acrylic colors, watercolors, and markers on my mixed-media pages.

2. Crumple up a piece of deli paper and glue it into a journal spread using matte medium. This simple layer gives my page some texture and later will allow fluid mediums to puddle and create beautiful patterns in the creases.

3. If your pages have some color on them, create a neutral base by covering both pages with white gesso or white acrylic paint. Gesso also acts as a primer for subsequent layers of paint.

   Paint a background. I love creating abstract shapes, varying the size, and adding some solid and outlined shapes.

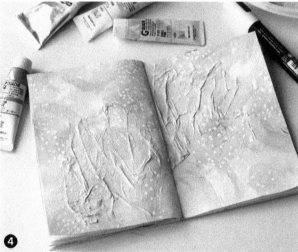

4. While the paint is still wet, add more depth by rubbing more paint into the outer edges of the shapes and blending them a bit with your fingers. Allow the pages to dry completely.

   Make marks with acrylic paint markers. I created dot designs, letting the pattern flow naturally over the entire page while making sure to leave some empty spaces.

5. Add a photo of yourself. I roughly cut out a black and white photo of myself.

   Add messy watercolors. After deciding where to place the photo, I brushed bright pink watercolor on the pages so it would surround the photo. Soften the edges with more water and swirl the paint around to make this layer look airy but messy. The gesso layer will prevent the watercolor from seeping into the paper.

6. Add more colors. I created depth with bright water-color in certain spots. Load the paintbrush with a lot of pigment mixed with water and allow the paint to drip across the page to enhance the messy look.

7. Draw several small flowers or leaves in black waterproof ink on a separate piece of paper and cut them out. Including simple illustrations like these gives your mixed-media art a unique look. Glue them around the photo using matte medium.

Draw more foliage on the background—this is an easy way to fill up empty spaces and create a flowing shape. You can also add more cut-out foliage to the pages.

8. Color the foliage with watercolor using messy brushstrokes.

9. To finish the piece, add a hand-drawn frame around the pages.

materials

- Two sheets of paper
- Cutting mat or an old, thick book
- Thin awl
- Needle
- Thread (I used unwaxed embroidery thread; stranded or pearl is fine)

Fiber and paper have had a long love affair. Instead of gluing one piece of paper to another, try this technique to sew them together, adding texture to your art.

1. Overlap the pieces of paper in a way that is pleasing to you and place them on the cutting mat. Use the awl to poke two rows of parallel holes on either side of where the two pieces of paper meet. Don't make the holes too small or they'll be difficult to sew through.

2. Thread the needle with the embroidery thread. Measure the length by doubling the length of the row of holes and adding a few extra inches.

   Starting on the underside of the paper, pull the needle through the bottom left hole and leave a 2" (5 cm) tail. Sew an X stitch: Push the needle diagonally from the front through to the next hole on the right. Bring the needle from the back through the hole straight across to the left.

3. Continue sewing this pattern until you reach the end, then sew back down the same way. Tie the ends together in a square knot on the back side of the paper.

4. Machine stitching is just as fun and looks just as nice as hand stitching. No special stitches are required; just make sure you stitch slowly and don't use glue to adhere the pages, which can damage your machine.

Add thread to your journals in loads of fun ways. Try changing the stitching pattern or use the technique on the edge of a page to create a border.

project LEFT BRAIN + RIGHT BRAIN = MIXED-MEDIA GRID

For this lesson in making a mixed-media grid, I'd like you to get particularly messy. We'll play like children with supplies and techniques and appease our creative, imaginative right brain. Then, we'll rein it all in to remind our analytical and methodical left brain that we love it, too.

materials

- Repurposed papers
- Mediums (paints, inks, acrylic texture mediums, oil pastels, etc.)
- Paintbrushes
- Palette knife
- Repurposed gift card or scraper

1. Grab a bunch of loose repurposed papers that aren't too busy; mine had black text. I always have vintage ledger and book pages lying around, but you might use letters from your kid's school, bills, and so on.

2. Gather a few different mediums; if your papers have color, choose mediums in the same color family. I chose white gesso and modeling paste, a few different types of paint in varying shades of pink, plus a beige oil pastel crayon and acrylic ink.

3. **Right-brain time:** Embrace your inner child and make marks on the page. Add your mediums to the page as a kid would, with inquisitiveness and curiosity and putting any self-criticism to the side. Paint with acrylics in big batches. Use paintbrushes, your fingers, a palette knife—anything you can get your hands on.

   Since the paper already has some interest to it, you don't have to fill the entire page with paint. If you find a particularly lovely image or text on the page, leave it as is.

4. Use the dropper from an acrylic ink bottle to make a flower shape. Use an oil pastel to create repeating marks and paint loosely with watercolor on the corner of a page.

MARK-MAKING IDEAS

Here are a few other ways to make marks on the page:

- Swatch your supplies (see page 35).
- Paint an entire page in one color or more than one color, using your fingers to blend the shades together.
- Use different tools to apply paint and mediums. Try brushes, an old gift card, a twig, or a carved potato stamp. Using a brush will give very different results than smearing paint on with an old gift card. You can also experiment with a twig as a brush or a potato cut in half as a stamp.
- Add modeling paste with a palette knife and level up by adding paint to color the paste (see page 86).
- Paint a thick layer of gesso on the page and, while wet, write into it with the back of a thin paintbrush.
- Draw or doodle your favorite shapes, images, or scribbles.
- Create repeating patterns using paint.
- Drop pigment onto the page with an eyedropper.
- Flick watered-down paint onto the page with a paint-brush or old toothbrush.

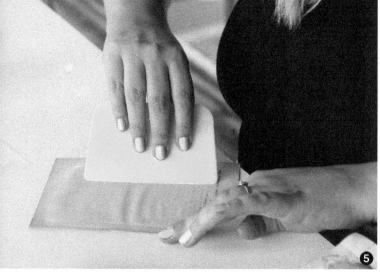

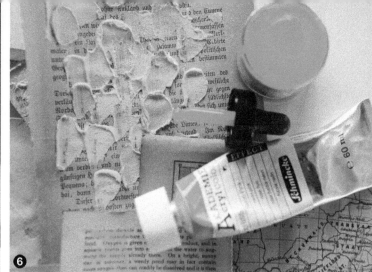

5. Go crazy with playing around. Smear on a thin layer of acrylic paint with an old gift card or scraper; this allows you to still see what's underneath. Write with the back of your paintbrush into gesso. Splash liquid watercolor. Use what you learned in chapter 2 to play with your supplies.

6. Add loads of texture; my favorite way is with modeling paste. Add color to it with paint or ink and spread it onto the paper with a palette knife, similar to frosting a cake.

7. Left-brain time: Cut the decorated papers into equal-sized squares. Crop them to create interesting little bits.

8. Arrange the squares into a grid that makes you happy (see the finished grid on page 72). Use both sides of your brain and follow your intuition to decide where they need to be placed. Balance heavier squares with squares that feel lighter. You can leave the grid as is or add lettering or ephemera to the top to bring it together.

Guest Artist
FRANCISCA NUNES

Do something small every day

Francisca Nunes is a mixed-media artist living in Portugal. She's passionate about art journaling and loves being free to create messy and intuitive art through mixing color, texture, and natural elements. Nature has an important presence in her work—she uses natural colors to eco-print the papers and fabrics that make up her art journals, in which she gets messy.

Instagram: @franciscanunes_heartmakes

Not having time is a common belief that prevents us from sustaining a consistent art practice. Regular creative practice gives you the joy and experience needed to grow as an artist. The materials you'll need for this project include a large piece of art paper sturdy enough to handle paint and collage, and whatever art supplies you have on hand.

1. Underpaper—what you put underneath your work to protect your desk—is where all the swipes of paint end up when you clean your brushes and doodle. This underpaper is the place where you don't overthink; it's the place made to be messed up. This is what makes it a great surface on which to create every day. On your underpaper, you are free and personal, which helps develop your style.

2

2

3

2. Your underpaper should be a large piece of paper. Play as if you are a child—free and fearless. Paint, doodle, and make marks and scribbles. If you don't like it, rip it up. And if you like it, rip it up anyway!

I invite you to develop a daily routine of creating little pieces of art each day. Add them as elements to your art journal, collage the bits, and create a bigger piece. You can also just keep the pieces as they are—they're already art.

3. Once you run out of space on your underpaper, rip it into different shapes with irregular edges. The more imperfect these shapes are, the more you'll feel free to play without self-imposed rules.

4. You'll end up with a great collection of tiny papers, already painted and doodled, calling you to continue creating.

PLAN AHEAD FOR PLAY

If you're cultivating a daily practice, save time by gathering some supplies in advance. Keep them at hand so you can play without spending too much time thinking about the techniques or materials you'd like to use. I love to use bits of underpapers, parts of my eco-dyed papers, magazines, and old book pages to create with collage. Store these in a box.

Even if you don't have time to create an entire spread in your art journal every day, you can grab a piece of paper from your box and continue the creative process. You only need a few colors, pencils, and mark-making tools or stencils to enable you to play a little bit every day.

5. Now it's time to collage, paint, and doodle. Be as free as you'd like. Don't overthink the process, and remind yourself that it's just a fragment of paper. Work on more than one piece at a time, and do something different each day: doodle, collage, paint. After a while, you'll have a collection of artful pieces.

Collage a small piece in your art journal as an embellishment or use it as a starting piece to create an even larger work. After days of consistent creative practice, you'll notice that your style will start to appear, and you'll feel more confident and freer to create.

project HAND-CUT LETTERING

Cutting letters from paper makes me feel like a kid again. Making these letters cursive makes the technique more grown-up. If you don't feel like writing out your thoughts or if you'd like to focus on certain words, give this a go.

materials

- Paper, such as magazine pages, wrapping paper, scrapbook paper, or leftover paper from previous projects (sheets from the mixed-media grid project [see page 72], supply swatches [see page 35], or paper decorated with modeling paste [see page 86])
- Scissors
- Glue

The paper left over from cutting out your lettering is also worth using.

1. Cut out a word or phrase in cursive from a piece of paper; I cut out "OK." The trick to making this whimsical and unique is to avoid using stencils or sketching the word in pencil. Let your scissors guide you. If you need a reference, write the word on another piece of paper.

② ③

2. Decide where you want to glue the word or phrase
    into your journal. I adhered mine to a piece of
    vintage wallpaper that was already bound into
    my journal. If you're not using a Messy Journal
    (see page 38), glue it to another sheet of paper.
    This technique works well on plain paper, but
    you can elevate it by using an additional piece
    of patterned paper.

3. Add extra journaling in the blank space on the page.
    Keep your writing loose and underline it without
    using a ruler.

project HOW TO LOOK
LIKE YOU KNOW HOW TO DRAW

materials

- Variety of pen types of your choice (see step 1)
- Reference image or live drawing subject
- Paper, including repurposed paper, such as an old book or ledger page

So many of us equate being an artist with being able to draw. Instead of learning to draw, I prefer being lazy and finding a hack.

This project, which features contour drawing, is a hack.

It encourages you to loosen up and focus on the act of drawing rather than the result. Because you know it's not going to be a realistic sketch, you release a lot of self-imposed expectations. This is also a great project if you're tightly wound, like me.

1. Choose a pen that offers little control; I like working with a brush pen. Find a subject to draw, preferably something or someone who is still, or a reference image. Look at your subject (flower, person, dog, coffee mug) and draw it without looking at the paper.

   You'll have strange lines—but you're supposed to. You'll have leaves coming out of the petals and that will become part of the charm of the drawing.

2. Keep playing with contour drawing. Choose another pen and hold it loosely. I drew with a Sharpie, an ordinary ballpoint pen, a watercolor marker, and an acrylic paint marker.

3. Draw on top of a photo. Colorful paint markers create great contrast on black and white images.

Guest Artist
ROBEN-MARIE SMITH

Messy and loose abstract foundations

Note from Caylee: In this tutorial we'll take an outside-in approach to art journaling. Using an assortment of art supplies you'll paint, make marks, and collage. Then you'll learn the process for breaking down that piece and giving it new life as you incorporate it into your journal and add finishing touches.

Roben-Marie Smith has been a working artist for the last sixteen years. As a self-taught artist she believes that anyone can cultivate their creative spark. Her work has been featured in several books and magazines, and she has taught mixed-media art workshops at retreats across the U.S. As a tech-savvy artist, instructor, and woman of faith, Roben-Marie's mission is to serve others and help them get the most out of their art as a hobby or as a business.

Instagram: @robenmarie

Art journaling is the place I go to experiment, play, and make mistakes while I document my life. The visual nature of art journaling is what drew me in many years ago. It's the perfect method for expressing my creative side while working through life's ups and downs.

materials

- Watercolor paper
- Art board
- Masking tape
- Pencil
- Watercolor
- Soft pastels
- Instant espresso granules
- Spray bottle filled with water
- White gesso
- Water-soluble art pencils and crayons such as Stabilo Woody 3-in-1 Colored Pencils
- Black Stabilo-All Pencil
- Small ephemera scraps
- Sewing machine or needle and embroidery thread

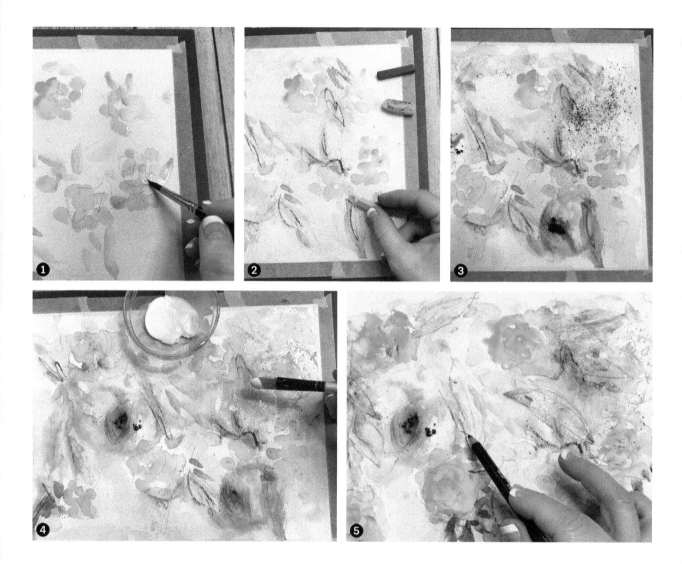

1. Tape down a piece of watercolor paper to an art board with masking tape. This minimizes the paper buckling when applying watercolor. Add pencil marks and watercolor splatters to the paper to create messy, abstract florals.

2. While the watercolor is still wet, add some marks to the design with soft pastels. Rotate the paper for different perspectives as you work.

3. Sprinkle instant espresso coffee granules in a few spots and lightly spritz with a water bottle.

4. Mix white gesso with a little water to create a wash. Lightly brush the gesso in random spots around the design.

5. Add abstract shapes and random marks with watercolors and water-soluble pencils and crayons.

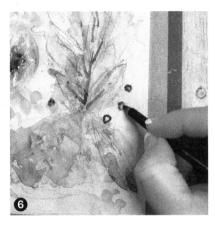
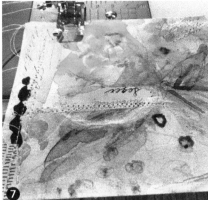
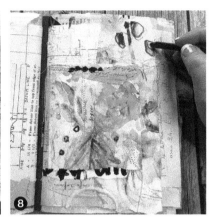

6. Create another layer of shapes and marks with pastels and watercolors. Add marks with white soft pastels. Create more marks with a Stabilo black pencil dipped in a little water.

7. Once dry, gently peel the tape off the watercolor paper and cut the paper into medium to small pieces. Gather an assortment of small ephemera pieces and collage them onto one of the cut pieces, adding hand or machine stitching with embroidery thread.

8. Adhere an assortment of papers to a journal page to create a background that complements your collage piece. Add the stitched collage piece as a focal point. Add finishing touches to the page with pencil and crayon marks.

MAKING THE MOST OF YOUR ART JOURNALING

· Scan your art before cutting it. I always scan my work so I can print and use it in other projects. I also use the scans to create digital art pieces.

· Don't be afraid to mix several mediums together. I love using pastels with water and acrylics with watercolors. Experiment and have fun!

· Take process photos as you create. These can be used later for inspiration, instructional tutorials, and content for social media.

project MODELING PASTE:
THE FROSTING ON THE ART CAKE

materials

- Stencil
- Low-tack, removable tape
- Coffee-dyed paper (see "Dyeing Paper with Coffee" sidebar)
- Modeling paste
- Acrylic paint
- Palette knife

1. Decide where on the paper you want the stencil image. Attach the stencil to the paper with tape to hold it in place while you apply the modeling paste.

2. Mix a small amount of modeling paste with some acrylic paint using a palette knife. The more paint, the more vibrant the color. Mix until fully blended and no streaks are visible.

Modeling paste is by far my favorite art material. I used to be a prolific cupcake baker and loved buttercream frosting. I love modeling paste because it feels like I'm working with that frosting again. Smearing it onto the page really is like putting the frosting on the (art) cake.

Modeling paste (also called molding paste or texture paste) is an acrylic-based texture medium that comes in regular and light weights. Light modeling paste dries more quickly than regular but is not as sturdy. You can use either type for this project.

3. Spread the colored modeling paste across the stencil with the palette knife. Make sure all the gaps are filled. Remove any excess paste with the palette knife, creating a fairly even spread.

4. Slowly peel the stencil from the paper while the modeling paste is still wet, making sure the stencil pattern is intact. Try not to tear the paper as you remove the tape. Immediately place the stencil in warm water so the modeling paste doesn't harden, rendering the stencil unusable. If you're lazy like I am, place the stencil between two baby wipes to keep it moist until you're able to clean it.

5. Don't let leftover colorful modeling paste go to waste. Create ephemera by using the paste with other stencils on sheets of paper. You can then use these decorated papers in your journals. Use white modeling paste on white paint for a tone-on-tone look.

DYEING PAPER WITH COFFEE

Fill a large, flat tray with water. Add a sprinkle of instant coffee granules and mix until dissolved. For a deeper color, add more coffee. Place a sheet of paper in the water, making sure it gets saturated. Once it's fully submerged, take it out of the water, remove the paper, and leave it to dry on a towel for a few hours or overnight.

The paper's color will depend on the ratio of coffee to water and the type of paper. Older papers, such as vintage book pages, may tear easily when wet, so handle with care. Experiment with how much coffee you add and different papers to get a variety of shades from light tan to walnut.

Once the paper has completely dried, it's ready to use.

3

CULTIVATE

CULTIVATE YOUR ARTISTIC PRACTICE AND TAKE YOUR CREATIVE LIFE TO THE NEXT LEVEL

We sometimes think that once we've made the first step and created something, the next time we make art it will be effortless.

It may get easier, but it's never easy.

Creating becomes part of you, but every time you sit in front of your journal, there may be some resistance. Just because you become good at something doesn't mean you'll be good every single time.

The reason for this is that life is full—and sometimes it gets in the way. Don't get sad about that. Too much life means you're living.

This trail shows you how to fit art into your messy, beautiful life. Over time you'll become great at figuring out exactly which barriers to creating life throws at you and what you need to equip yourself with to break them down. In this trail I'll discuss the main barriers to creating and share how you can overcome them. We'll turn our weaknesses into strengths.

project THE IDEA NOTEBOOK

When you don't know what to make, check out the projects in the "Spark" trail (see page 49).

When you don't know how to make something, check out the projects in the "Grow" trail (see page 61).

When you have too many ideas . . . Oh, honey, of course you have too many ideas. You're a glorious creative unicorn who never stops thinking about how you can turn that coffee shop interaction into art. You see every Instagram post as an invitation to try out a new technique. You're an artist.

Creating an idea notebook is the solution for managing a head full of ideas.

Creating an idea notebook is a great way to manage having too many ideas and to combat having too few ideas. These are not opposing problems. You might think that you could never not have ideas, but you're wrong. I love you, but you're wrong.

An idea book is for contributing and taking ideas.

The book should be a small, softcover notebook that is never decorated or customized. Write in it with a plain pen. It is the opposite of Instagrammable.

It needs to be damn ugly. A gorgeous book can distract you from putting your ideas on the page.

Use this idea notebook as your brain's external hard drive. You can store all your ideas there, leaving your brain free for creative idea generation. When you have an idea, a technique you'd like to try, even a spark of an idea, write it in your book. Get in the habit of writing in it.

Your idea book needs to be with you everywhere (that's why it needs to be small), and you should get in the habit of writing in it.

You can also use digital idea books; even a note-taking app on your phone will work.

Putting your ideas on paper not only helps you remember them, but it also makes them objective—you're no longer thinking, *"Damn, that's silly,"* or *"I'll never be good enough to try that."* You're looking for a spark. When you turn something creative into a to-do list item, you're able to act. You're no longer starting from zero.

TURN YOUR FEELINGS INTO ART

Note from Caylee: Part of growing as an artist is creating art that is close to what you see in your mind. A good practice for this is creating intuitive art.

When Connie Solera taught for Get Messy for the first time, I was in awe of her students' work.

I believe she was put on this Earth to make everyone better and truer artists. She teaches art that allows you to follow all that you are—even your perceived weaknesses—and encourages using this technique to connect with your soul. This project will help you do that.

Guest Artist
CONNIE SOLERA
Painting as affirmation

Connie Solera is devoted to a daily creative practice of drawing, painting, and art journaling. Her art embraces the unseen, scratches at life's mysteries, and explores the deeper, darker spaces of her being. As a teacher with more than twenty-five years of experience, Connie loves to guide her students through the same explorations.

Instagram: @conniesolera

When I created this page, I was busy with all kinds of things and I wanted to express that creatively. Here is how I made my busy mind visible.

Your art journal will never judge you, no matter how you feel or what you think. Art journaling is an awesome way to affirm how you feel, clear away any energetic debris, and keep a visual journal of your own inner life journey.

My approach to art journaling is simple: show up and let my feelings direct my mark-making and creative decisions. Returning to this simple process has strengthened my trust in myself and deepened my connection to my creativity tenfold.

I encourage you to think of your art journal as a sacred space. Think of the blank page as a trusted friend who relishes in your beauty, messiness, and imperfect perfection of who you are and who you are becoming.

All of you are welcome in the pages of your art journal. This is a private place for you to express your fear, your rage, and your delight. Art journaling is not about getting it right or making a perfect picture. Our mission is to show up, make marks, feel, release.

materials

Note: I encourage you to gather whatever supplies you feel most comfortable with. No expertise in art making is required. Make sure your supplies are within reach.

- Acrylic paint
- Paintbrushes
- Oil pastels
- Water-soluble graphite

1. Place your hands on a spread in your journal. This is the first thing I do when I come to the blank page; this is how I center myself. As my hands gently move across the paper, I set an intention that the marks I am about to create are an affirmation of where I am right now in my life and how I am feeling. This is my safe space.

2. Choose a paint color that catches your eye, pick up a brush that does the same, and make a mark. No matter how I'm feeling or what kind of day I've had so far, this first mark always makes me happy. Let this first mark help you sink into yourself and remind you how safe you are to express and explore in your art journal.

   What do you notice about how you're feeling? When you look at your art supplies, what color or supply is calling you now? Where does your attention go? Do you want to keep using the same color and materials or change things up? Feel free to lay down large areas of color, slap down some patterns, or even play with a line. There is no way to get this wrong. Make a mark and then make another. Trust how you feel.

3. Pick up an oil pastel. Holding an oil pastel is different from a paintbrush and reminds me of coloring as a child. Activating that muscle memory helps me create lines that are childlike and expressive. If you feel like switching up materials, go for it. But notice how using that material makes you feel.

4. Take a moment to check in while you're painting. Maybe you notice a tinge of anger. What color does your anger yearn for? What does your anger want to do with that supply? Scribble? Make aggressive lines? Draw an ugly face? Put it on paper and affirm how you feel.

I usually reach for water-soluble graphite when I feel something intense. When I hold it, I can't stop the urge to come at my page with a bit more force. Water-soluble graphite is messy when activated by water or paint, and that messiness is the perfect reflection of how I feel.

Sometimes when we paint as affirmation, the page might look like a hot mess. That's totally okay. I believe a hot mess is getting more bang for our buck!

Don't let an intense feeling pass you by—make art from it. How can you make it the muddiest disaster you've ever seen on paper? How does that feel? Do you feel lighter? Are there more marks you want to make?

5. Invite your fingers to the party. I grabbed a jar of army green paint and smeared it on the page.

Applying paint with my fingertips allowed me to drop into a blissful state—I love that the most about painting. Don't be surprised if you start a page feeling one way and go through a spectrum of feelings as you progress. Remind yourself that expressing these parts of yourself is sacred.

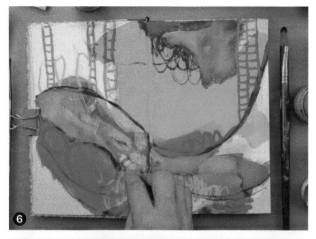

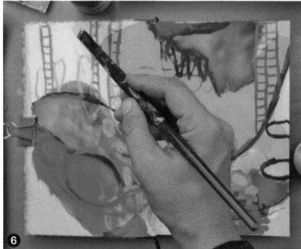

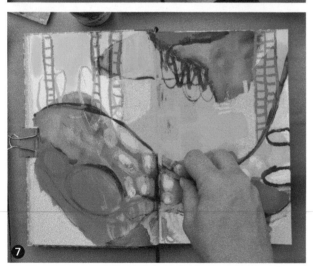

6. Let's address the inner critic who might show up as you make your way through painting as affirmation. When your inner critic starts nibbling away at your experience, don't panic. Look at your painting and choose one little thing that's working or feels good. Go back to the place that felt good to create.

   Sink into how you feel and trust that you can transmit that feeling into your painting one mark at a time. Your goal is not to create something recognizable, pretty, or logical, so tell your inner critic to sit this one out and return to feeling your way through your painting process. You've got this.

7. This is as far as I can take you. When you're engaging in painting as affirmation, all you need to do is show up, make a mark, feel, release, and repeat.

   It sounds easy-peasy, but this approach to art journaling requires us to be curious about how we feel and where those feelings are in our bodies. For those of us who care for a family, spouse, or our community, shifting that focus inward can be challenging. So please be gentle with yourself and know that it's totally okay to make art journal pages that look and feel like hot messes or complete mud pies. It doesn't mean something is wrong with you or that you're a horrible artist. It simply means that you are getting out the junky-junk and making it easier for the good stuff to flow through later.

   I promise you, painting as affirmation can transform your life. Open your art journal, pick up your brush, and give it a try!

materials

Note: Create a faux travel supply kit. We're not going anywhere, but this will help remove decision paralysis and allow you to create more and think less (yay!).

- Small brochure or pamphlet with a few pages
- White gesso
- Scraper or craft spatula
- Double-sided tape or glue stick
- Scrap paper and ephemera
- Watercolor
- Paintbrush
- Acrylic paint
- Optional add-ons: Writing tools, ink, gouache

You live a full, beautiful life. Part of that is not having much time for anything other than that glorious life you're living.

When my son was a newborn, I experienced the greatest time deficit of my life. When I don't make art, I get cranky. I couldn't shake the fact that I needed to create something to get some crankiness out of my system. That's when I came up with a journal in one sitting.

When you treat a journal as a whole, filling it becomes less intimidating. You also lower your expectations—it doesn't need to be world-changing, it just needs to be completed in a day. When you focus on that, you stop overthinking. You channel your inner wisdom, learn to trust it, and act on it.

No more excuses, okay? Okay.

Find a small brochure or pamphlet with just a few pages to use as your journal—working small is the best tip for filling up a journal as quickly as possible.

Make some coffee and get started.

1. Cover up anything in the brochure you don't love with white gesso, using a craft spatula or scraper, and creating an even layer on the page. Tear out pages you don't like or glue them together. You can also glue scrap paper, ephemera, or pieces of your own artwork to cover up pages and form a base to work on.

When using gesso, be sure to make a mess of it and get it all over other bits of the brochure. This is an easy way of making things look more artsy.

2. Page through the brochure (which is now your journal) and look for areas to enhance; perhaps one section looks pale compared with another section's bright blue. Treat the journal as a whole rather than working on individual spreads. Work in layers randomly throughout the journal. As soon as you begin to question what to do next, turn the page.

MAKE USE OF TOOLS THAT MAKE THE PROCESS FASTER

- **Scraper or craft spatula:** Create a thin layer of gesso that dries quickly.
- **Fingers:** Use with paint or gesso and work intuitively.
- **Paper:** Fold and tear it rather than fussing with scissors.
- **Ephemera:** Use precut pieces.
- **Quotes and phrases:** Use text that you've saved in your idea notebook (see page 90).

3. Decorating the cover of a journal is usually done right at the beginning, but I would like you to try it out somewhere in the messy middle. Since the middle is where the magic happens and the cover is the face of your journal, harness that magical time for the bit that counts the most.

   When you're working with a technique you love, put that on the cover too. I like the tactile feeling of gesso on my fingers, and the cover of this brochure had some embossing with an interesting texture; I knew it was cover time. Add a favorite piece of ephemera on the front as well.

4. Add the next layer to the journal pages; I added an abstract painted design using what I call a smooshing technique (a good technique to have in your back pocket for time-limited journaling). Work on a gessoed page. Add a lot of water to the brush and create uneven pools of water on the page. Dip the brush in watercolor and add the paint to the pools. When the paint dries, some areas will be more translucent, and some more opaque.

5. Add ephemera to the pages. Follow your heart and intuition but try adding a larger piece of paper to a relatively bare page, or pair a neutral image with a bright one. Smear some acrylic paint on multiple busy images to create balance.

6. Use other parts of the brochure, such as torn-out pages. Cut out images and place them in a new position, crop images, or group them together. Add lettering. Continue to look through the pages to find areas to work on until you feel the journal is finished.

You can use your journal as a base for more artwork or as a completed piece of art. You've created what you need, and you're definitely no longer cranky.

TURN YOURSELF INTO ART

Note from Caylee: The ultimate masterpiece that can never be beaten is the artist. You are glorious.

Everything you put into your journal comes from you, but adding yourself to your journal is a way to document who you are at that instant, a snapshot of your universe at a particular moment in time.

When I look at Lynissa's art, I immediately understand her more. The way she uses herself in her work endears me to her. I asked her to share a practical way for you to do the same.

Guest Artist
LYNISSA HAYES

Layers of the self

Art is a passion for Lynissa Hayes, an independent, fun-loving artist from Houston. Art journaling is an expression of that passion. Growing up as an only child and an introvert, she's used her creativity to freely communicate her ideas, faith, and voice to the world. Her art journals are a reflection of her many creative pursuits over the years including painting, photography, sewing, paper crafting, mixed media, and more.

Instagram: @makers_ave

There is nothing flat about people. We're multilayered individuals who play different roles in our everyday lives while expressing a wide range of personalities and characters. This tutorial reflects that layered dimension. While working with mixed media, collage, and personal images you'll explore layering techniques that allow you to self-reflect while creating in a way that's free-flowing and intuitive.

materials

- Selection of printed papers, scrap papers, and ephemera
- Images, including photos of yourself
- Adhesive of your choice
- Cutting tool (scissors, paper punch, craft knife, circle cutter, etc.)
- Cutting mat
- Optional add-ons: stapler, acetate or vellum, mark-making tool (acrylic paint pens, permanent pens, markers, etc.)

1. Gather images and background papers you want to work with, including photos of yourself. Use scratch paper with swatches of colors, scribbles, handmade marks and doodles, or painted papers made from monoprints stenciled with modeling paste. This is the perfect time to experiment and play.

2. Choose a blank journal spread. Adhere the papers to both pages, creating a collage. Cut out a shape from one of the pages using scissors, a punch, or a craft knife. Place a cutting mat underneath the page if cutting into the page. I cut a circle in the middle of the left-hand page using a circle cutter.

3. Adhere another piece of paper to the back of the cutout. Don't limit yourself to just paper; I adhered glitter tulle to a piece of cardstock, which added texture.

4. Cut your portrait out of the photo. Fold a few sheets of paper in half that are larger than the photo and stack them together with the folds to the left. Place the photo on top with the image facing up and hold everything together with a sturdy clip. Cut along the edge of the photo and through the papers with scissors, making sure not to cut through the folds. Create a booklet for journaling by nesting the papers together, one inside the other.

5. As an option, add more dimension by layering acetate or vellum on top of the photo and adhering with a stapler or dot of wet glue. Trace or make marks on top with acrylic paint pens, permanent pens, or markers.

6. Gather your selection of printed papers, scrap papers, and ephemera, and attach them to the spread with an adhesive of your choice. Double-sided tape works well at keeping chunkier paper glued in. Add embellishments to finish the page; I added beads, word stickers, and paper die-cuts. Use materials or words that reflect your mood and personality.

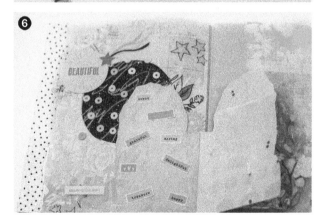

These techniques can be used together or separately for more minimal layouts. Don't overthink the design and go with the flow. Focus on celebrating yourself and the many aspects and layers that make up your wonderful self!

ARTIST DATES: WOO YOUR ARTIST HEART

I maintain a great relationship with my husband and myself through dates. To make someone fall in love with you, you woo them; you can do the same for the artist inside of you.

The artist inside you is looking for a bit of a spark.

When you give her some excitement, she'll give some back in your art.

Artist dates are the way to practice that artist self-love.

project EXPLORE AND DRAW

Explore and draw is one of my favorite artist dates to take myself on. As you saw in the lesson on blind contour drawing (see page 82), I am not an expert at drawing. That inexperience is what makes this project even more fun. If you're good at drawing, I encourage you to forget that fact so that you can embrace the freedom of a beginner. Take what you learned in the blind contour lesson and apply it to this project.

1. Get all dressed up as you would for a regular date. Wear your favorite dress, wash your hair, and wear that sparkly eye shadow. Put your journal and some limited art supplies into a bag.

   I brought a few journals but felt drawn to an altered book that had pages covered with gesso.

2. Draw something near where you live. This can be an entire building or a detail that caught your eye. I like the repetitive nature of buildings, especially castles, so that's what I drew.

   Make a blind contour drawing of your subject (where you don't look at your page until you're finished) or a semi-blind drawing (where you peek every now and then). I did the latter for this castle.

3. If you feel stuck creating your drawing, try sitting in a new position. The point of the illustration is to get a feeling of the place, not to create a scientific diagram of your surroundings. I used a brush pen to keep my drawing loose and imperfect. You can also try drawing with your nondominant hand or using a crayon to find that freedom in being imprecise.

   While creating, take note of your environment. Practice mindfulness by blocking out everything that isn't your art or your heart. You can add to your drawing when you get home, or declare it finished. One of the objectives for this type of artist date is to look and record the feelings that came with what you saw.

MORE IDEAS FOR ARTIST DATES

My other favorite artist dates include:

- **Going on a photo walk.** Choose a theme (a color, a shape, signs, doors, etc.) and take photos of things that conform to that theme.

- **Enjoying a piece of your favorite cake at a café.** Save all the paper bits (menu, business cards, pamphlets), and add them to your journal.

- **Taking a class.** This can be art-related, but it doesn't have to be.

- **Being a tourist in your own neighborhood.** Visit an art museum and take it all in. Go to one of your town's tourist traps and view it as if you've never been there before. Rediscover the wonder of your area.

- **Looking at flowers.** If you don't have a garden, visit a communal or public garden. Photograph yourself among the flowers.

- **Reading a creative book.** If you'd like accountability, create a book club and discuss it with a few friends.

- **Meditating.** Follow a guided meditation or sit in silence with your own thoughts for ten minutes. Follow your meditation with a cup of tea.

- **Going to a library.** Choose a book to digest simply because it looks beautiful. I love pop-up libraries where people leave their old books.

- **Remember:** It doesn't matter what you do, only that you do it.

Categories don't need to be perfectly aligned. This game is meant as a guide, so if things don't quite fit, just be more creative.

TIGER TIME

Tiger Time is a special, dedicated time for creating. I call it this because of the power in starting your day with making art. By waking up a little earlier, you're creating the space for art in your life and prioritizing your creative practice.

Here's how to do it:

- Set your journal and supplies out the night before so they're ready to go.

- Set your alarm for thirty minutes before your usual wake-up time.

- Don't check your phone when you wake up and keep it on "Do Not Disturb" mode while you work.

- Go to your art space and create for thirty uninterrupted minutes.

THE BLANK PAGE

Being a creative person doesn't have to be lonely, but art is made alone. Even if you're creating among friends, the ultimate decision of whether to create or not to create is yours alone. In the end, it's just you and your journal, whether you're a blossoming beginner or prolific pro.

There may be times when you'll feel frozen, when you'll stare at that blank piece of paper and it looks back at you with its stark white face. Your ideas are rolling around your mind like tumbleweeds or exploding like fireworks. It can be tough to decide which path to follow. All you need to do is get some momentum going.

Here are my hacks and tricks to beat the blank page:

- Introduce yourself to your journal. Document who you are on the page at this moment. Jot down the date, your age, and where you are in life. Bonus points for a photo (I love passport photos for this).

- Skip the first page of the journal. If it feels like a lot of pressure to make the first page perfect, begin your journal on the second page.

- Jump around. Who says you have to work in consecutive pages? You're not writing a book, so give yourself that freedom.

- Don't start from zero. Bind your own book by following the instructions in "Creating Your Messy Journal" (see page 38) and include pages with text, patterns, or color.

- Create an idea notebook (see page 90) so your idea-generating and art journal pages are separate. Use the notebook as a to-do list.

- Remember your "why." Make a note in your journal about why you journal. Allow yourself to remember why you started.

- Use loose, messy handwriting to empty your thoughts onto the page. Once you've started moving, you can paint, collage, and create art on top.

- Stop when you're full. Usually we create until we're empty. Part of Ernest Hemingway's daily writing routine was coming to a place where he knew what to write next and then stopping. He'd come back in the morning ready to go. This can be tough to achieve, but it's a surefire way to beat the fear of the blank page.

TURN YOUR LIFE INTO ART

Note from Caylee: Including yourself in your journal is not just about your selfies. Your life is art. Your decisions are art. Your art journal is a place to store who you are at that season of your life. Who you are changes over time, but you're able to go back to those moments of time.

Johanna Clough is an artist who excels at translating life into art. She takes seed packets, children's art, sofa fabric samples, movie ticket stubs, and perfume packaging and turns them into art. Whoa.

Guest Artist
JOHANNA CLOUGH

Translating life into art

Johanna Clough is a journal maker, mother, and memory keeper from New South Wales, Australia. She has a passion for journaling about her life and her family's life as a way to keep a time capsule. She loves making journals that inspire others to document their lives.

Instagram: @johannaclough

Apart from making handmade journals, I'm also known for filling them with precious memories and mementos from my life. I've always been inspired by vintage scrapbooks, the kind with ephemera stuck onto the pages accompanied by little notes and annotations. I love old scrapbooks that hold greeting cards, beauty packaging, food packaging, locks of hair, invitations, photographs, and more.

Each day I am truly mindful about my life: What do I want to document, and how can I do that creatively? Most of the time, ephemera pops up naturally and is easily attainable.

Keeping ephemera is keeping history, documentation, and evidence of where we've been and what we've done. There is also the fun, arty, creative, visually appealing, and limitless joy of being selective with our supplies, patterns, and colors. The two go hand in hand when journaling in a meaningful way.

I find it fascinating to look at these old items and imagine all the memories and stories attached to them. My junk journals are a modern-day version of ephemera keeping. I like to think that what I hold on to will be interesting in the future for me, my family, and anyone else who may view it. I've kept pieces of my life for as long as I can remember, but the passion for putting them into books accelerated after having children, as did my creativity and the limits of what I keep. I learned that through scrapbooking, or journaling in a creative way, I can showcase an array of elements from the story itself, including the emotions behind it, and my thoughts and ideas for both past and present.

Benefits of incorporating real-life pieces in your journaling and art include giving pages substance and purpose, keeping pages relevant through sentiment, creating art that's meaningful or relevant to others, creating a time capsule or piece of history, and developing your creativity and art skills.

Here are my how-tos for making the most of ephemera pieces from your life:

- Don't feel as though you have to keep everything. Ask yourself, is this something with memories surrounding it? Is it visually appealing, or can I make it so? Will it be interesting in twenty years? If you answer no to any of these questions, don't keep it.

- Think about the senses when you look at ephemera: What are you seeing, smelling, hearing, tasting, or touching? Is there anything tangible attached to that? If you still feel there is nothing, take a photo. Be inventive: draw a picture, have someone you love write a note, quote something that was said, or pick a flower or plant to press.

- Collect things when you're busy and sort through them later. I often throw my ephemera in a drawer and when I have time, I sort through them to decide what should be kept and how.

4

CONNECT

CONNECT WITH A COMMUNITY THAT GETS YOU AND YOUR ARTY AWESOMENESS

Have you ever been in your art studio or workspace and wanted some company? Have you ever longed for someone to lift you up during an artistic burnout, to talk louder than your inner critic, or to cheer you on when you have more ideas than time?

Me too.

That's why Get Messy exists.

Community brings a dedicated space to ask questions, share your unbridled enthusiasm for your favorite type of glue, and discuss living a creative life with others who are trying to do the same.

Magic happens when you build a friendship based on art and when you build an art habit based on friendship. When you mix art and community, you're almost guaranteed that magic.

Part of magic is not quite understanding how it happens. All I know is that I've seen the magic happen. Repeatedly.

This trail is the level up for all the other trails.

BUILD COMMUNITY AND FIND YOUR CREATIVE HOME

There's no reason to be stranded on an arty deserted island all by yourself. A community of creatives is waiting to connect with you.

If you are in a tiny German village, as I am, you can still find your creative family through the power of the Internet.

Here are some easy ways to create community:

- Join an established creative community (Oh, hey, like Get Messy!)

- Join an online class and spend time in the Facebook group.

- Join Instagram and share your work.

- Use a hashtag (add an applicable one when posting your work, search them on Instagram, or follow a few to see new artists. #getmessyartjournal is clearly my favorite).

- Comment on other people's Instagram posts.

- Start a book club.

- Reach out to an artist you admire and ask to collaborate on a project or creative challenge.

- Join a creative challenge such as the "100 Day Project" or the "Get Messy Habit" (making a conscious effort to create something small at a consistently frequent interval).

- Collaborate via a round-robin journal, where one or more journals is sent to a group of artists who contribute their work.

- Create art on a postcard and send it to someone.

- Swap either your artwork or some collected ephemera with another artist (also called an art swap).

- Join an accountability group or find an accountability partner.

- Give, give, give. Give your likes and compliments freely. Be a cheerleader for other creatives. This is how you put some juju in your karma bank and what will have you receiving some too.

HOW COMMUNITY LEVELS UP YOUR CREATING

I asked some of the loudest cheerleaders in the art journaling community to share their experiences with art journaling, community, and the interlinking of the two. As a bonus, they share their art as well.

DEBBIE BAMBERGER

Community never judges

Debbie is a sexual and reproductive health nurse practitioner in Berkeley, California. When she discovered art journaling in 2016, it changed her life. In addition to raising teen sons, fighting for reproductive and racial justice, and nurturing her twenty-year marriage, she art journals every day, inspiring others to do the same.

Instagram: @debbiebamberger

Discovering art journaling touched something deep. I tried written journaling intermittently over the years, but it never stuck. Art journaling, though, felt transformative.

Two components of art journaling are particularly meaningful to me. I can dive deep into my emotions—anything that's troubling me or that I'm thinking about—and explore and process those on the page through painting, collage, scribbling, writing, drawing, or mark-making. The art doesn't have to look nice or make sense or be readable. But it helps me make sense of things.

The second component is the online art journaling community. I found a community of friends, supporters, and cheerleaders. I have formed deep and lasting relationships with my art friends, many of whom I have never and may never meet in person. I committed to making art in a journal every day three years ago, and my community encourages me, holds me accountable, and never judges. I can now say four words that never crossed my lips prior to age 50: I am an artist.

CHARLENE DeROUIN

Art journaling gives you a voice to tell your story and community enriches your journey

Charlene is an artist, designer, and maker whose work is abstract, intuitive, and organic, with a no-rules approach. She is influenced by experiences and emotions, colors, patterns, and just about anything that sparks creativity. Charlene loves art journaling for its personal expression and connection with others.

Instagram: @charderouin

Art journaling is where you can speak your truth and express feelings through visual art and the written word. Art journaling is personal; it's not a one-size-fits-all kind of thing. It's a trusted repository, a safe place without judgment. You decide what to share with others. This can also be a place to try new techniques and document your creative practice. An art journal is whatever you want it to be. There are no rules.

The art journaling community includes some of the most supportive and generous people I know. We love to share, encourage, collaborate, and connect, and not just our work. We exchange information about classes, techniques, supplies, and anything else that enriches the journey. No matter where you are on that journey, you'll find the support you need if you just reach out.

Art journaling has given me a voice to tell my story. I can't imagine life without it.

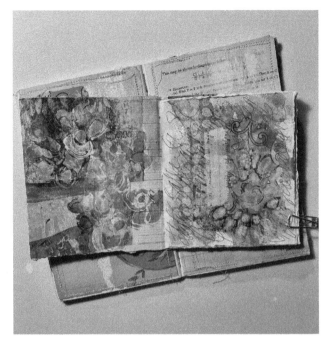

ROSE SHERIDAN

Purpose for lonely days

Rose is the mother of a seven-year-old human and a twelve-year-old Jack Russell terrier. She is a lecturer in psychology and child development at a U.K. university and considers herself a lifelong learner. Art journaling is her magic.

Instagram: @rosieraindrops

My art journal is my equivalent of a secret garden. The little girl enters the garden moody and carrying all kinds of emotions, and the garden helps her process her thoughts and feelings and creates purpose during her lonely days. In the same way, my journal helps me make time for myself, in a world where everyone seems to want a piece of me. I can channel negative or difficult emotions into art and, in doing so, my mood improves. I need to make art to be the best mother, wife, friend, daughter, and teacher that I can be.

The art journaling community provides me with friends who are encouraging and supportive of my art. Being able to chat with friends while creating is lovely. I can get advice, encouragement, or sympathy from others who are trying to find time to put themselves out there and create art that's meaningful and beneficial. I started art journaling to claim some creative time for myself as a new mother, but I stuck with it because the community lends me kindness, strength, and light. My art is elevated because of the safety net that the community provides. I know there will be support, advice, and encouragement in response.

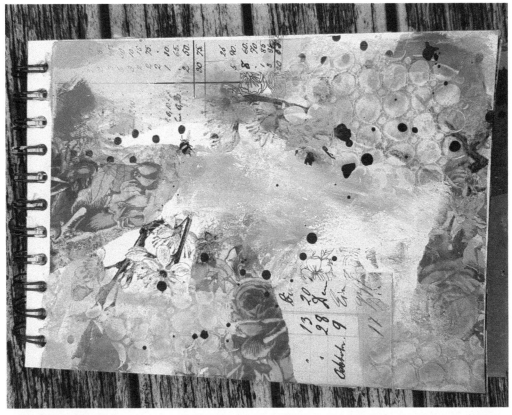

ALYSSA GRIESE

The nudge to take a chance

Alyssa lives in Canada and has a bachelor's degree in visual arts. She is a maker and lover of all things handmade. For Alyssa, embracing imperfections and chasing after happy accidents is the true magic of art journaling. Anything goes within the pages of her art journal, and her journal has become an important place for her to process, experiment, and play.

Instagram: @thistleandthimbles

I first started an art journal because I needed a place to let my creativity flow. I hadn't painted or done anything creative in a long time, and my art journal quickly became the place where I would let myself play with ideas and techniques. There was no pressure because it wasn't meant for anyone to see, and it wasn't for sale—it was just for me.

Then, I discovered this lovely little art journal online community called Get Messy. Members would give one another prompts or challenges for their art journals and share their work within the community. I lurked as an outsider for quite a while before deciding to participate. I was nervous to share something that was originally meant only for me, but the whole vibe of the community was very welcoming, so I took a chance. I've never looked back.

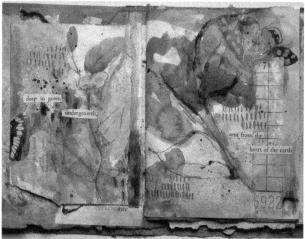

Having a community filled with artists who want to play and explore and grow with you has changed everything I thought I knew about art. The support you get from sharing your work, ideas, or experiments with people who have similar goals and interests has been unmatched. This keeps me motivated to continue creating and trying new things. Sometimes just showing up to your work and starting can be the most difficult thing to do. Knowing that I have this wonderfully supportive community behind me gives me that extra nudge to put my pencil on the page and make something.

MEAGAN FUNK

Finding courage in community

Meagan lives in Montana where she spends summers adventuring outdoors and winters hibernating indoors with her art supplies. Meagan is inspired by nature and loves to incorporate it into her art journal pages. She journals to help calm her mind and keep herself sane.

Instagram: @meaganelizabethart

I've always been a creative person, dabbling in many types of art. I discovered art journaling a few years ago and instantly fell in love with it. It was a way to combine my creative loves into one place. Art journaling has no rules. Having a journal and making art in it is all that's required. I love that the work I create doesn't have to be a masterpiece or shared with anyone. And if I don't like it, I can turn the page and move on.

Art journaling is one of the few things that can get me into a state of flow and turn off my overactive monkey brain for a while.

I art journal because I need to be creative. I need it to keep me sane and happy. I've also found a community of like-minded artists I can share my journey with. An entire community of people around the world gets as excited about art supplies as I do. I can ask them questions, and they'll cheer me on. I've met amazing friends through the art journaling community, and I am constantly inspired by them. They give me the courage to keep going and creating. I've learned that art is for everyone. The hardest step is often just starting. I have to remind myself daily to sit down and begin, but once I do, magic happens.

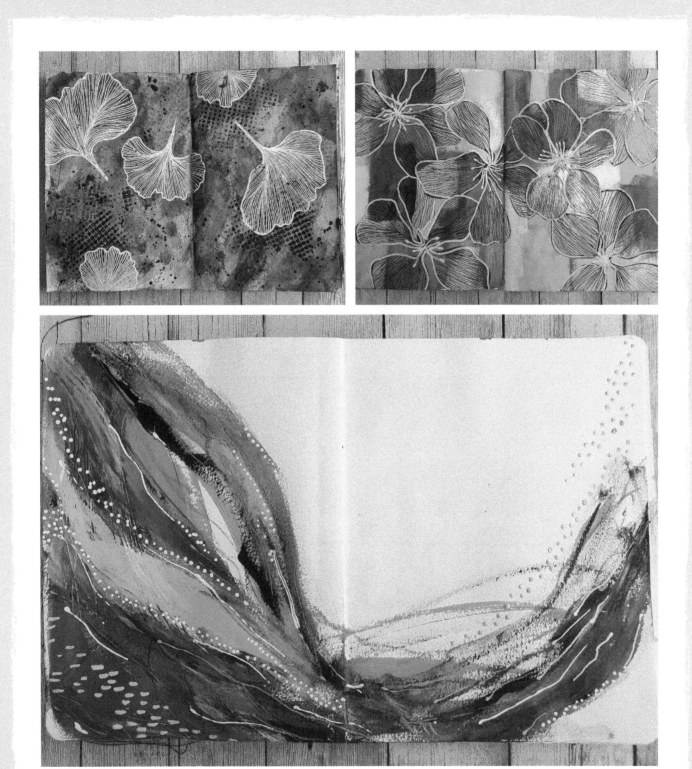

VANESSA OLIVER-LLOYD
@dansmoncrane

"Art journaling is a way of processing feelings and thoughts and pouring them into a container (the journal) that can then be closed and put away—or opened and revealed to all."

MEREL DJAMILA
@mereljournals

"Documenting your travels is one of the most fun things to do. You don't have to travel all over the world to discover beautiful places; you can discover new treasures in your own city. I imagine myself flipping through my journal in thirty years and seeing my drawings and writings and thinking about the memories that I have because I put them down on paper when they were still fresh in my mind."

MISTY GRANADE
@misty.granade

"I stumbled into art journaling sideways while showing up every day. I love books. I love making books. I love the idea of the permanence of keeping art in a book so it's part hidden secrets, part adventure you can explore over and over again. It's thrilling to look at an art journal. It can be literally anything. And to me that's the perfect encapsulation of us as individuals. There's so much magic just inside the covers."

GILLY WELCH
@gillywelch21

"My happy place is when I'm creating in my art journal, usually by sticking down random scraps of paper or adding special memories to the books I'm making for my granddaughters. Some days I may only manage ten minutes; however, even that amount of time is enough to make a difference, and it's important for my well-being and state of mind."

Resources

Creative community

- @getmessyartjournal on Instagram and #getmessyartjournal to find creative friends
- Joybook is a wonderful space to hone in on the journaling side of art journaling: https://joybook.life/
- Get Messy Art: https://getmessyart.com
- The Get Messy Art podcast: https://getmessyart.com/podcast/

Handmade journals

- Willa Journals binds journals that make me all warm and fuzzy. She has classes on how to bind them too: https://www.instagram.com/willa.wanders/
- Johanna Clough is the Mama of Junk Journals and sells limited editions through her Little Bindy shop: https://www.littlebindy.com/
- Sources for vintage books to use as art journals: eBay, Etsy, thrift stores, flea markets, garage sales

Art supplies

- Ceramicist Saara Kaatra creates adorable confetti paint palettes: https://www.etsy.com/shop/Piecesofporcelain
- I love cork pencil bags for an eco-friendly way to carry supplies around: https://fairkorkst.de/
- Moleskine journals: https://us.moleskine.com/en-us
- Kuretake pens and brush pens: https://www.kuretake.co.jp/en/product/brushpen/
- Golden paints: https://www.goldenpaints.com/
- POSCA paint markers: https://www.posca.com/
- My favorite place for twine: https://www.garn-und-mehr.de/
- Moriah Costa creates handmade watercolor paint in the most gorgeous shades (including a Caylee Grey signature palette of neon pink and titan buff!): https://www.etsy.com/shop/Illustratedmyrh

Acknowledgments

To T. Obviously.

To Elliot, for filling up my time with so much happiness that there's just no room for anything other than productivity.

To Jeannine, my own personal fairy godmother.

To Kelli, for helping me relearn the lessons I've already learned in art in other areas of life.

To Deb, for the voice notes, hilarious stories, and help avoiding squirrels.

And most of all, to the Get Messians. Always.

About the Author

CAYLEE GREY is a South African artist living in Germany. Her favorite title is Fairy Artmother, but she's also partial to wife and mama.

Caylee's life mission is to empower as many amazing, real-life humans as possible to get into a regular creative practice.

Caylee started making art in 2013 as a way to fight against her default states of laziness and passivity. Art constantly enables her to be deliberate and goal driven. Action is what helps her keep depression at bay.

She has absolutely zero formal training in art. Caylee wouldn't have even said she was creative until she started actively working in her art journals. Her technical work is rooted in the combined knowledge of the Get Messy community—Messy Artists have taught her everything she knows. As an immigrant, almost all her work revolves around finding a sense of belonging. The rest revolves around connection, and, predictably, identity.

Her favorite technique is collage. She believes in making a whole bunch of average art in order to get to the good stuff and actively practices dancing naked in perfectionism's face.

Index

Printed in the USA
CPSIA information can be obtained
at www.ICGtesting.com
LVHW061030240923
757412LV00069B/490